BLACK & DECKER®

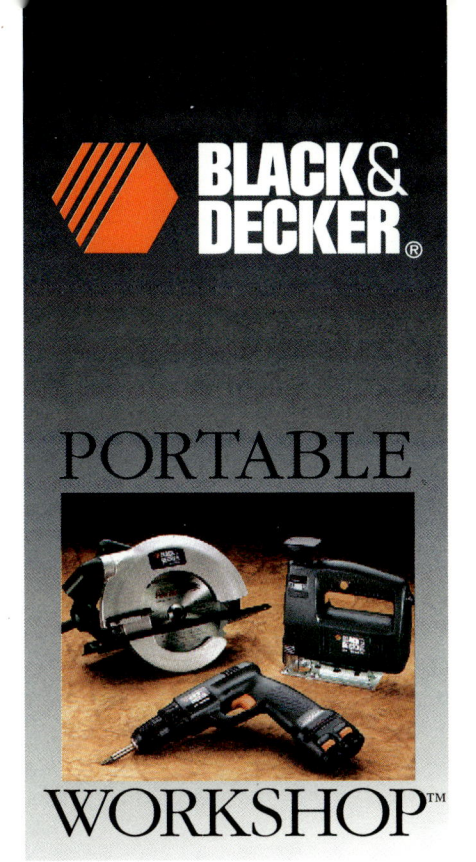

PORTABLE WORKSHOP™

Basic Wood Projects with Portable Power Tools

Vacation Home Furnishings

COWLES Creative Publishing
A Division of Cowles Enthusiast Media, Inc.

Credits

Copyright © 1996
Cowles Creative Publishing, Inc.
Formerly Cy DeCosse Incorporated
5900 Green Oak Drive
Minnetonka, Minnesota 55343
1-800-328-3895
All rights reserved
Printed in U.S.A.

COWLES
Creative Publishing
A Division of Cowles Enthusiast Media, Inc.

President/COO: Nino Tarantino
Executive V.P./Editor-in-Chief:
 William B. Jones

Executive Editor: Paul Currie
Project Director: Mark Johanson
Associate Creative Director: Tim Himsel
Managing Editor: Kristen Olson
Project Manager: Lori Holmberg
Lead Project Designer: Jim Huntley
Editors: Mark Biscan, Andrew Sweet
Editor & Technical Artist: Jon Simpson
Art Directors: Ruth Eischens, Gina Seeling,
 Nick Vlcek
Technical Production Editor: Greg Pluth
Project Designer: Rob Johnstone
Technical Art Draftsman: John T. Drigot
*Vice President of Photography
 & Production:* Jim Bindas
Copy Editor: Janice Cauley
Shop Supervisor: Phil Juntti
Lead Builders: Rob Johnstone, John Nadeau
Builder: Troy Johnson
Production Staff: Carol Harvatin, Laura Hokkanen,
 Tom Hoops, Gary Sandin, Mike Schauer,
 Brent Thomas, Greg Wallace, Kay Wethern
Studio Services Manager: Marcia Chambers
Photo Services Coordinator: Cheryl Neisen
Lead Photographer: Rebecca Schmitt
Photography Assistant: Dan Cary
Production Manager: Stasia Dorn

Printed on American paper by:
 Inland Press 99 98 97 96 / 5 4 3 2 1

COWLES
Enthusiast Media
President/COO: Philip L. Penny

Created by: The Editors of Cowles Creative Publishing, Inc., in cooperation with Black & Decker. ●BLACK&DECKER® is a trademark of the Black & Decker Corporation and is used under license.

Library of Congress
Cataloging-in-Publication Data

Vacation home furnishings.
        p. cm.—(Portable workshop)
 At head of title: Black & Decker.
 ISBN   0-86573-673-1 (hardcover).

1. Furniture making--Amateurs' manuals.
I. Cy DeCosse Incorporated.
II. Black & Decker Corporation (Towson, MD)
III. Series.
TT195.V33   1996
684.1--dc20   96-30485

Contents

Introduction 4
Tools & Materials 5

Projects
Deck Chair 8
Fireplace Box 12
Trash Can Protector 16
Modular Couch 20
Cottage Clock 26
Cedar Bench 30
Dock Box 34
End Table 38
Changing Screen 44
Cabin Marker 48
Cabin Porter 52
Field Kitchen 56
Cabin Chair 62
Ski Rack 66
Dart Board Cabinet 70
Lap Trays 74
Gun Cabinet 78
Suitcase Stand 84
Boot Dryer 88
Rod & Tackle Center 92

Introduction

That old orange recliner with the torn upholstery; the hand-me-down picnic table held together with wire and duct tape; the clock radio with the missing light and the ripped speaker... vacation homes always seem to become repositories for the worn-out, broken and out-of-style furnishings that are no longer welcome in our primary residences. And that's understandable. No one wants to spend a lot of money furnishing a cabin, cottage or chalet that may only be used a few weeks out of the year. But in *Vacation Home Furnishings* from the Black & Decker® Portable Workshop™, you'll find a host of low-cost alternatives to the rusty, wobbly TV trays you found lying around in your basement. Included in this book are 20 clever vacation-home projects you can build yourself with only the most basic power and hand tools—you don't need to be an experienced woodworker to make them. If you own a second home, or know someone who does, this is the project book you've been waiting for.

A folding ski rack you can put right outside your chalet door; a sturdy cedar bench that is amazingly easy to build; a decorative changing screen that livens up any room and can provide some much-needed privacy. These are just three of the innovative projects you'll discover in *Vacation Home Furnishings*.

For each of the projects in *Vacation Home Furnishings*, you will find a cutting list, a materials-shopping list, a detailed construction drawing, full-color photographs of the major steps, and clear, easy-to-follow directions that guide you through every step of the project.

The Black & Decker® Portable Workshop™ book series gives weekend do-it-yourselfers the power to build beautiful wood projects without spending a lot of money. Ask your local bookseller for more information on other volumes in this innovative new series.

NOTICE TO READERS

This book provides useful instructions, but we cannot anticipate all of your working conditions or the characteristics of your materials and tools. For safety, you should use caution, care, and good judgment when following the procedures described in this book. Consider your own skill level and the instructions and safety precautions associated with the various tools and materials shown. Neither the publisher nor Black & Decker® can assume responsibility for any damage to property, injury to persons, or losses incurred as a result of misuse of the information provided.

Organizing Your Worksite

Portable power tools and hand tools offer a level of convenience that is a great advantage over stationary power tools. Unlike stationary saws and drills, they can be thrown into your trunk, along with some basic building materials, and be used to create projects from wood anywhere you go. But using them safely and conveniently requires some basic housekeeping. Whether you are working in a garage, a boathouse or outdoors on your dock, it is important that you establish a flat, dry holding area where you can store tools. Set aside a piece of plywood on sawhorses, or dedicate an area of your workbench for tool storage, and be sure to return tools to that area once you are finished with them. It is also important that all waste, including lumber scraps and sawdust, be disposed of in a timely fashion. Check with your local waste disposal department before throwing away any large scraps of building materials or any finishing-material containers.

If you are using corded power tools outdoors, always use grounded extension cords (called *GFCI* cords), connected to a grounded power source.

Safety Tips
- *Always wear eye and hearing protection when operating power tools and performing any other dangerous activities.*
- *Choose a well-ventilated work area when cutting or shaping wood and when using finishing products.*

Tools & Materials

At the start of each project, you will find a set of symbols that show which power tools are used to complete the project as it is shown (see below). You will also need a set of basic hand tools: a hammer, screwdrivers, tape measure, a level, a combination square, C-clamps, and pipe or bar clamps. You also will find a shopping list of all the construction materials you will need. Miscellaneous materials and hardware are listed with the cutting list that accompanies the construction drawing. When buying lumber, note that the "nominal" size of the lumber is usually larger than the "actual size." For example, a 2 × 4 is actually 1½ × 3½".

Power Tools You Will Use

Circular saw to make straight cuts. For long cuts and rip-cuts, use a straight-edge guide. Install a carbide-tipped combination blade for most projects.

Drills: use a cordless drill for drilling pilot holes and counterbores, and to drive screws; use an electric drill for sanding and grinding tasks.

Jig saw for making contoured cuts and internal cuts. Use a combination wood blade for most projects where you will cut pine, cedar or plywood.

Power sander to prepare wood for a finish and to smooth out sharp edges. Owning several power sanders (⅓-sheet, ¼-sheet) is helpful.

Belt sander for resurfacing rough wood. Can also be used as a stationary sander when mounted on its side on a flat worksurface.

Router to cut decorative edges and roundovers in wood. As you gain more experience, use routers for cutting grooves (like dadoes) to form joints.

Guide to Building Materials Used in This Book
• Sheet goods:
PLYWOOD: Basic sheet good sold in several grades (from CDX to AB) and thicknesses. Inexpensive to moderate.
BIRCH PLYWOOD: A highly workable, readily available alternative to pine or fir plywood. Moderately expensive.
GROOVED PLYWOOD SIDING: Exterior plywood sold in 4 × 8 sheets; front has vertical grooves, usually 4" or 8" apart. Inexpensive.
TILEBOARD: Thin sheet good, often called shower board, that is coated and very water-resistant. Inexpensive.
• Dimension lumber:
PINE: A basic softwood used for many interior projects. "Select" and "#2 or better" are suitable grades. Relatively inexpensive.
CEDAR: An excellent wood for outdoor building projects. Highly resistant to rot. Has a rustic appearance that makes it a good choice for many vacation homes. Inexpensive to moderate.

Guide to Fasteners & Adhesives Used in This Book
• Fasteners & hardware:
WOOD SCREWS: Brass or steel; most projects use screws with a #6 or #8 shank. Can be driven with a power driver.
DECK SCREWS: Exterior screws that work well with softer wood, like pine and cedar, and with sheet goods. Sold in a variety of lengths and with several different types of rust-free coatings.
NAILS & BRADS: Finish nails can be set below the wood surface; common (box) nails have wide, flat heads; brads or wire nails are very small, thin fasteners with small heads.
MISC.: Door pulls & knobs, butt hinges, loose-pin hinges, plastic or nylon glides, barrel locks, hasps, piano hinges, strap hinges, snap catches, lawn mower wheels with steel-rod axles, other specialty hardware as indicated.
• Adhesives:
WOOD GLUE: Yellow glue is suitable for most interior projects.
MOISTURE-RESISTANT WOOD GLUE: Any exterior wood glue, such as plastic resin glue.
CONSTRUCTION ADHESIVE: Sold in cartridges; provides water resistant bonding for sheet goods.
• Miscellaneous materials:
Wood plugs (for filling counterbores), dowels, wallpaper, battery-operated clock, decorative trim moldings.

Finishing Your Project

Before applying finishing materials like stain or paint, fill all nail holes and blemishes with wood putty or filler. Also, fill all voids in any exposed plywood edges with wood putty. Sand the dried putty smooth. Alternative: fill counterbored pilot holes with wood plugs if applying stain. Sand wood surfaces with medium-grit sandpaper (100- to 150-grit), then finish-sand with fine sandpaper (180- to 220-grit). Wipe the surfaces clean, then apply at least two coats of paint (enamel is most durable), or apply stain and at least two coats of topcoating product. Always use exterior-rated products for outdoor projects.

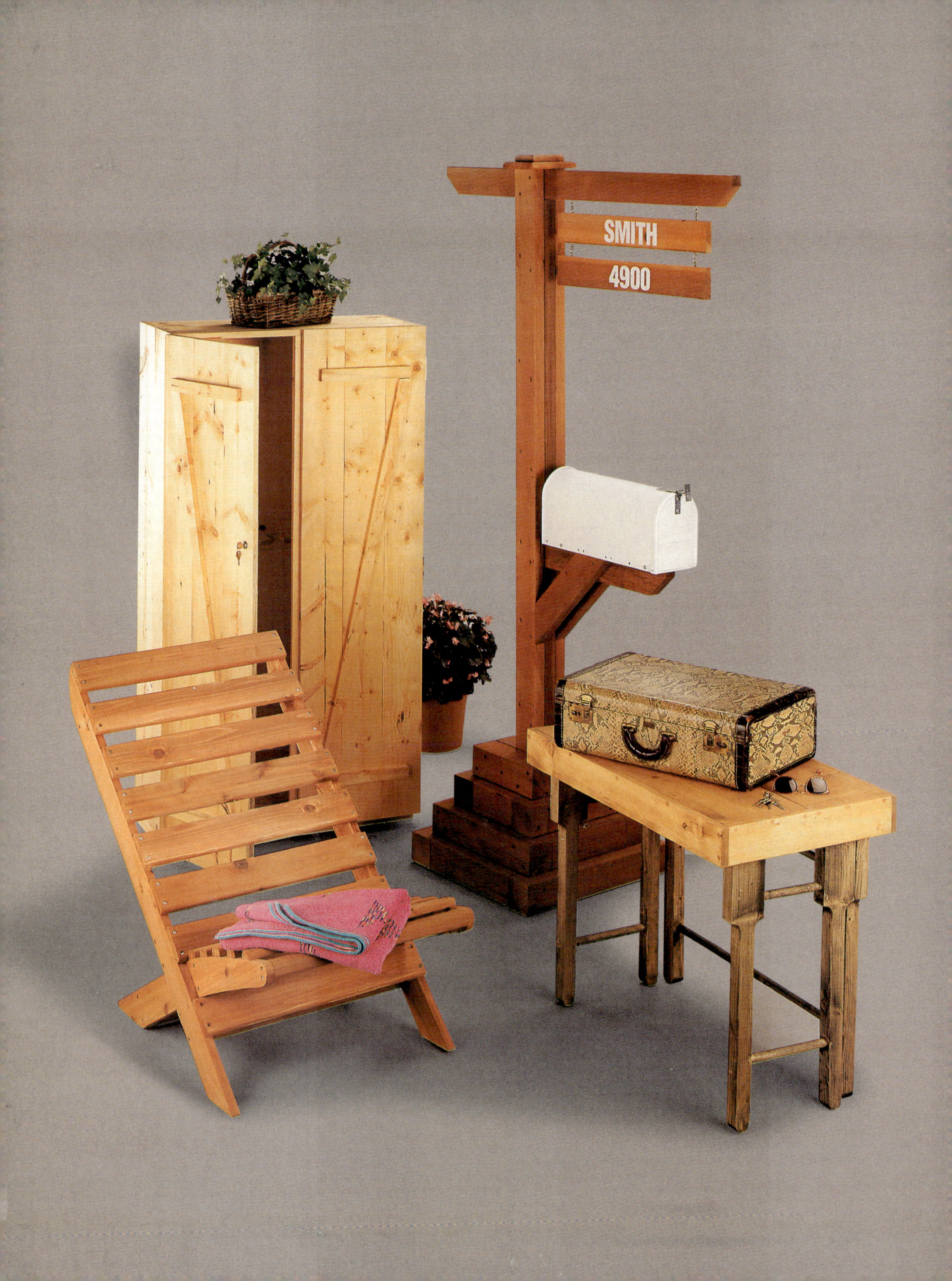
SMITH
4900

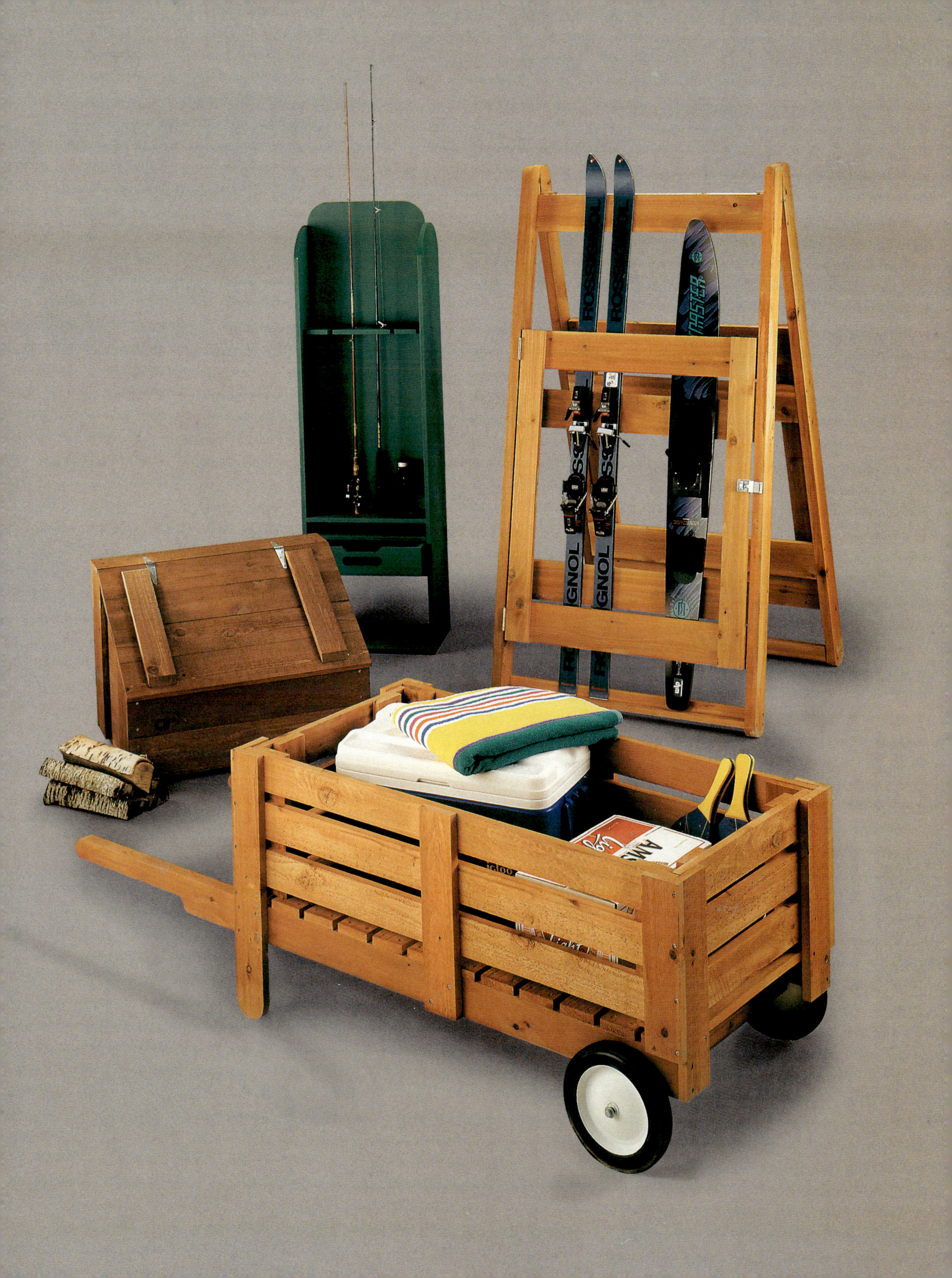

PROJECT
POWER TOOLS

Deck Chair

Lean back and soak in the sun on this supremely comfortable cedar chair for your deck or for the beach.

Construction Materials	
Quantity	**Lumber**
2	1 × 2" × 8' cedar
5	1 × 4" × 8' cedar
1	1 × 6" × 6' cedar
1	2 × 2" × 6' cedar

Angled perfectly for sunbathing on a deck, in the yard or at the beach, this sturdy, comfortable beach chair is one of the cleverest and most convenient pieces of outdoor furniture you can find. This deck chair is made of two parts that disassemble easily and quickly for storage or transport. The long back section is a simple frame made with sides, slats and stretchers. The seat section fits between the back slats to create a stable, versatile chair. When the sun goes down, just pull the seat section out, slip it into the back section, and carry it away. When you lean back and enjoy the sun, you will be amazed at how comfortable this chair really is, and how easy it was to build.

8 VACATION HOME FURNISHINGS

OVERALL SIZE:
35" HIGH
24" WIDE
40" LONG

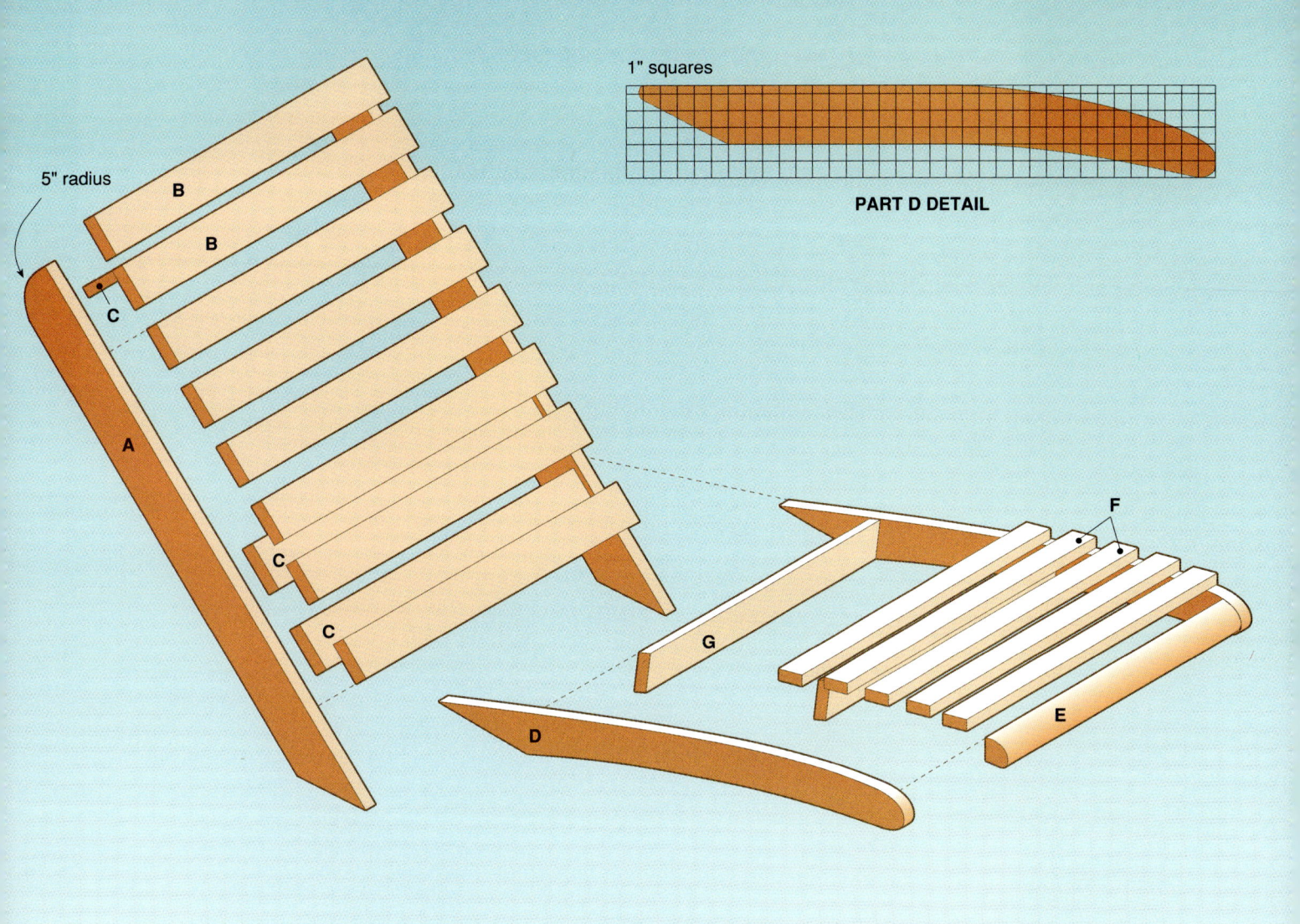

1" squares

PART D DETAIL

5" radius

	Cutting List			
Key	**Part**	**Dimension**	**Pcs.**	**Material**
A	Side	¾ × 3½ × 49"	2	Cedar
B	Back slat	¾ × 3½ × 24"	8	Cedar
C	Stretcher	¾ × 3½ × 22¼"	3	Cedar
D	Leg	¾ × 5½ × 35"	2	Cedar

	Cutting List			
Key	**Part**	**Dimension**	**Pcs.**	**Material**
E	Front spreader	1½ × 1½ × 20½"	1	Cedar
F	Seat slat	¾ × 1½ × 22¼"	5	Cedar
G	Stringer	¾ × 3½ × 20½"	2	Cedar

Materials: Moisture-resistant glue, deck screws (1⅝", 2"), finishing materials.

Note: Measurements reflect the actual thickness of dimensional lumber.

VACATION HOME FURNISHINGS 9

Directions: Deck Chair

MAKE THE SIDES. The sides are long boards that serve as the main structural members on both sides of the back frame. Each side is cut to shape with one slanted end and one curved end. Start by cutting the sides (A) to the length shown in the *Cutting List*. Clamp the sides together, edge to edge, so their ends are flush. To cut the sides to shape, first draw reference lines for the bottoms of the sides: at one end of each side, use a combination square to draw a straight line at a 45° angle from the inside edge corner toward the opposite corner, 3½" in from the ends. On the other end of each side, use a compass to draw a 5"-radius curve that forms the top (see *Diagram*). For large-radius curves, use a thin, straight piece of scrap wood as a homemade compass. First, mark the centers of each side, 5" down from the tops of the sides and 1¾" in from the edges. Drive a nail through the scrap piece on one centerpoint. Slide a pencil through a hole in the scrap piece, 5" from the nail. The curves should start at the top, inside corners of the sides and end on the outside edge, 4½" down from the top edge **(photo A)**. While the sides are still square, mark reference lines to help you position the two bottom slats and two bottom stretchers. Mark reference lines on the side faces, 7½", 8½", 14¾" and 15¾" up from the bottoms of the sides. These reference lines will be used later in the assembly process. Cut the sides to shape with a jig saw.

ATTACH THE BACK SLATS. Slats are attached on the front edges of the sides to form the back frame. Make sure you carefully align the bottom two slats with their reference lines before attaching them—the gap must be wide enough to accommodate the seat section. Begin by cutting the back slats (B) to size. Draw reference lines at each end of the slats, ⁷⁄₁₆" in from the ends. Drill two evenly spaced pilot holes through each reference line. Position the sides on their edges so the flat edges are facing up. Use glue and 2" deck screws to fasten one back slat at the top (curved) ends of the sides, making sure the edges are flush. Position two slats so they align with the reference lines 7½" and 14¾" up from the bottom (slanted) ends of the sides. The bottom edges of the slats should be flush with the lines. Attach the slats with moisture-resistant glue and 2" deck screws, making sure to maintain a 3¾"-wide gap between slats **(photo B)**. Then, starting at the tops of the sides, attach the remaining slats with glue and deck screws, using a scrap 1 × 2 as a spacer to maintain the gap between slats.

ATTACH THE STRETCHERS. The stretchers are attached between the sides to add struc-

A makeshift wood strip compass can be used to mark rounded cutting lines.

Position two slats so their bottom edges align with the reference lines, then attach them to the sides.

Fit the stretchers between the sides so they are flush with the rear edges, and fasten them with glue and screws.

10 VACATION HOME FURNISHINGS

Soften the sharp corners of the slats with a router and roundover bit or a sander.

Round over the front spreader to follow the profiles of the legs.

tural support and brace the seat section when it is fitted in place. Cut the stretchers (C) to size. Position the back frame on your worksurface so the slats are on the bottom. Fit one stretcher between the sides, 4½" in from the top (curved) ends, and fasten it with moisture-resistant glue and 2" deck screws. Make sure this top stretcher is attached so its long edges are flush with the edges of the sides. The remaining two stretchers are attached so their faces are flush with the back edge of the sides. Position these stretchers on the reference lines, 8½" and 15¾" in from the bottoms of the sides, and attach them with glue and 2" deck screws **(photo C).** It is crucial that these bottom stretchers be separated by a 3¾"-wide gap; otherwise, the seat section might not fit securely into the back frame. Round over the top faces of all the slats with a router and a ⅜"-dia. roundover bit **(photo D).**

MAKE THE SEAT SECTION. Cut the legs (D) to length. Draw a grid with 1" squares, and transfer the grid pattern from the *Diagram* on page 9 to the workpiece. Cut the leg to shape with a jig saw, and sand the edges. Trace the finished leg onto the uncut leg, and cut it to shape. The slanted end of each leg is the rear end, and sits flush against the floor when the chair is assembled. The front ends of the legs are slightly rounded so your legs will be comfortable. Draw reference lines across one face of each leg, 6" and 20" in from the back (slanted) ends. These reference lines mark the position of the stringers (G). Cut the stringers to size, and fasten them between the legs with moisture-resistant glue and 2" deck screws. The rear faces of the stringers should be flush with the reference lines. Countersink the screws so the screw heads are slightly recessed. Cut the front spreader (E) to size, and fasten it between the legs so the front edge is flush with the fronts of the legs. Use a belt sander to round the front spreader to match the curved profile of the fronts of the legs **(photo E).** Cut the seat slats (F) to size. Drill pilot holes at each end of the slats for 2" deck screws. Starting 1½" in from the fronts of the legs, attach the slats with moisture-resistant glue and deck screws, maintaining even spacing by using an unattached slat as a 1½"-wide spacer **(photo F).**

APPLY FINISHING TOUCHES. Finish-sand all the surfaces of the beach chair, taking care to smooth out any rough or sharp edges. Wipe the wood clean, then apply an exterior-rated finish to the project to preserve the wood. We used a redwood-tinted, exterior penetrating wood stain.

Use a scrap as a spacer for setting gaps as you attach the seat slats.

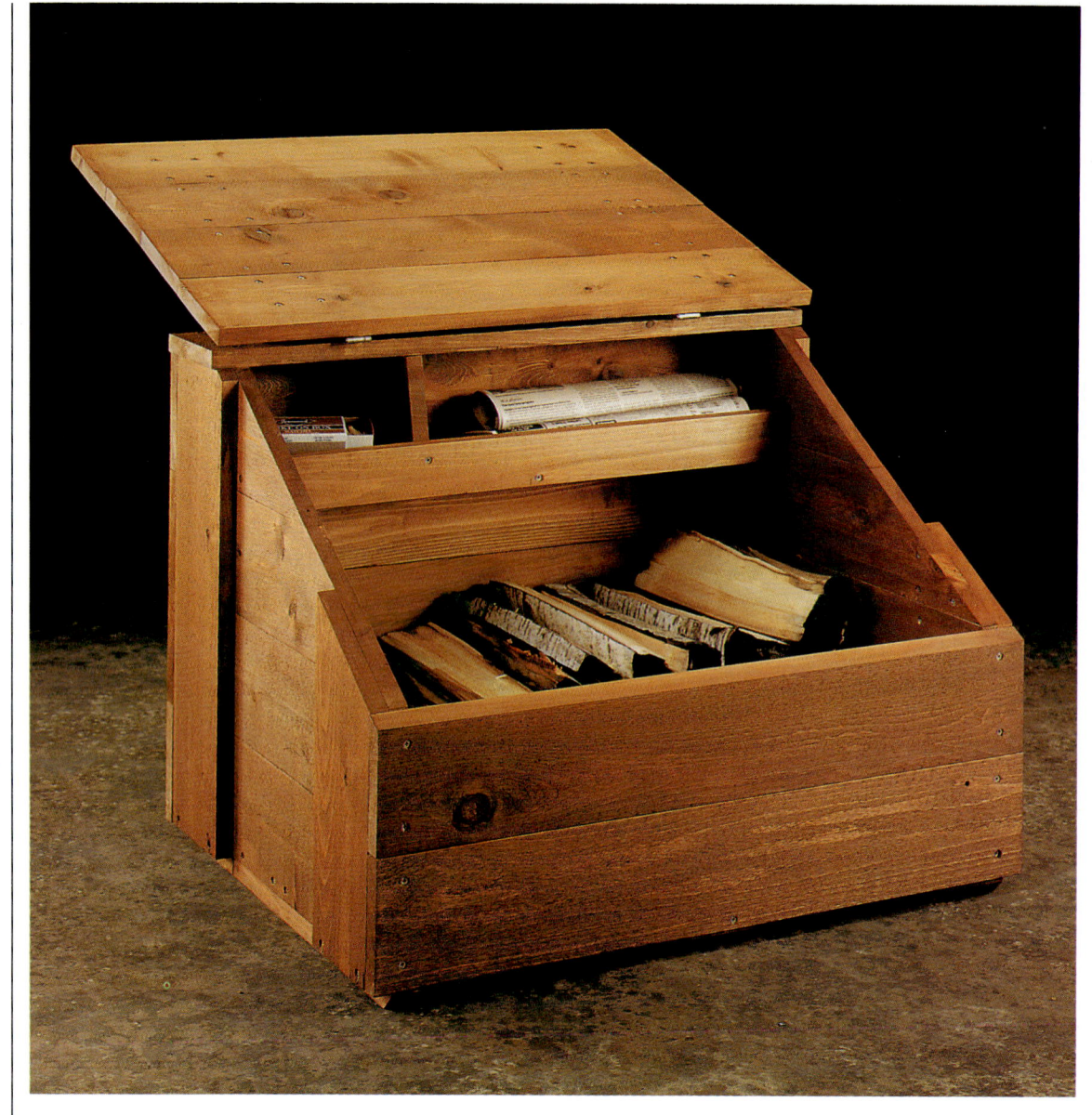

PROJECT
POWER TOOLS

Fireplace Box

This rustic firewood storage box nestles into your fireplace hearth, keeping all your kindling and cordwood in one neat package.

Construction Materials	
Quantity	**Lumber**
1	1 × 3" × 6' cedar
2	1 × 4" × 8' cedar
8	1" × 6 × 8' cedar

A simple storage box made from cedar, this fireplace box allows you to store your wood where it is needed—near the fireplace. It's an attractive project that looks great in any vacation home. The main compartment holds cordwood and kindling, and a handy shelf at the top is used to store tinder and matches.

We modeled this fireplace box after Early American styles, which served homes so reliably all those years ago. There was very little to improve upon; this project is easy to build and easy to look at. And if you have small children, you can even equip it with a hasp and lock to keep matches out of reach.

12 VACATION HOME FURNISHINGS

OVERALL SIZE:
23¾" HIGH
23¾" WIDE
31¾" LONG

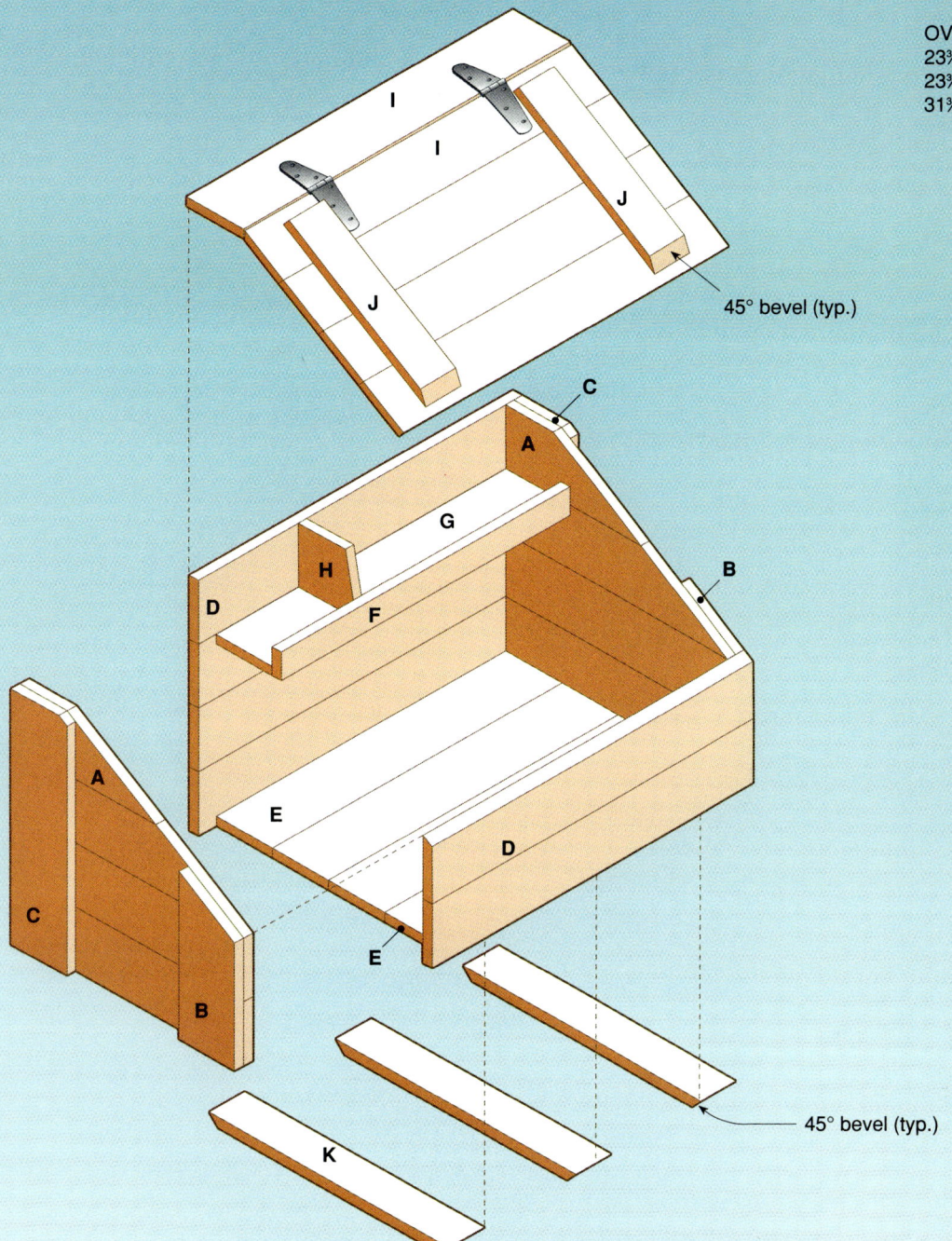

45° bevel (typ.)

45° bevel (typ.)

Cutting List				
Key	Part	Dimension	Pcs.	Material
A	Side board	⅞ × 5½ × 22"	8	Cedar
B	Front post	⅞ × 5½ × 15"	2	Cedar
C	Rear post	⅞ × 5½ × 22"	2	Cedar
D	Front/back	⅞ × 5½ × 31¾"	6	Cedar
E	Floor slat	⅞ × 5½ × 28¼"	4	Cedar
F	Shelf front	⅞ × 2½ × 28¼"	1	Cedar

Cutting List				
Key	Part	Dimension	Pcs.	Material
G	Shelf bottom	⅞ × 5½ × 28¼"	1	Cedar
H	Divider	⅞ × 5½ × 5½"	1	Cedar
I	Top board	⅞ × 5½ × 32"	5	Cedar
J	Support	⅞ × 3½ × 20"	2	Cedar
K	Skid	⅞ × 3½ × 23½"	3	Cedar

Materials: Deck screws (1⅝", 2"), 4" strap hinges (2), finishing materials.

Note: Measurements reflect the actual thickness of dimensional lumber.

VACATION HOME FURNISHINGS 13

Use a circular saw to make angled trim cuts in the box sides.

Use a belt sander to extend the slant of the sides onto the top edge of the front board.

Directions: Fireplace Box

MAKE THE SIDES. Each side of the kindling box is made by attaching four side boards edge to edge to form 22 × 22" square panels. After the sides are joined to posts at the top and bottom, each side is cut with a circular saw to produce the slanted profile of the box sides. Start by cutting the side boards (A), front posts (B) and rear posts (C) to size. Sand all parts after cutting to smooth out any rough spots. Clamp the side boards together in two groups of four, making sure the edges are flush. Position a front post and rear post at the ends of each group of side boards. The rear posts should be flush with the side boards at all edges, and the front posts should be flush with the front and bottom edges of the sides. Drive 1⅝" deck screws through the side boards and into the front posts and rear posts. Countersink the screws slightly to recess the screw heads, and unclamp the workpieces. To cut the sides to shape, draw a cutting line from the front edge to the back of each side. Mark the cutting lines, starting on the tops of the sides, 4⅝" in from the back edges, and running down to the top of the second lowest board at the front edge. Use a circular saw to cut along the cutting lines **(photo A)**. If any screws have been placed along the cutting line, remove them prior to cutting the sides.

ATTACH THE FRONT & BACK BOARDS. The front and back boards close in the box frame. Start by cutting the front/back boards (D) to size. Position two boards at the front of the sides, and four in the back. Attach the boards to the sides with 2" deck screws, driven through the front/back boards and into the sides. Use a belt sander to extend the slanted profiles of the sides onto the top board at the front of the box **(photo B)**.

INSTALL THE FLOOR SLATS. Cut the floor slats (E) to size, and fit them into the bin. Make sure the bin is square by checking the corners with a framing square. Adjust as needed. Fasten the floor slats to the bin by driving 2" deck screws through the bottom edges of the box and into the floor slats.

MAKE THE SHELF. The shelf fits in the top section of the bin and is used for storing matches and tinder. Start by cutting the shelf front (F), shelf bottom (G) and divider (H) to size. The divider has a slightly slanted front edge. To cut the divider to shape, mark a point on one edge, ⅜" in from one corner. Mark another point on an adjacent edge, 4⅜" away from the same corner. Draw a cutting line connecting the two points, and cut with a jig saw. Next, butt the shelf front against one long edge of the bottom. Make sure the ends are flush, and

TIP

Always make sure that firewood is dry and insect-free before storing it inside your home. One good way to help ensure that there are no big surprises hiding inside the wood you bring into your house is to store only split wood firewood in your storage box: generally, if wood is badly infested you will be able to see it when it is split into quarters or halves.

drive 2" deck screws through the face of the shelf front and into the edge of the shelf bottom. Position the divider on the shelf bottom, 8" in from one end. Make sure the slanted front edge of the divider faces the shelf front. Drive deck screws through the shelf bottom and shelf front, and into the divider. Place the shelf assembly in the bin. The top edge of the divider should be flush with the top edges of the box. Attach the shelf by driving 2" deck screws through the back and sides of the bin, and into the shelf edges **(photo C).**

MAKE THE LID. Cut the top boards (I) and supports (J) to size. Fasten one top board to the top of the bin so the back edges are flush and the top board overhangs the ends by ⅛". Drive 2" deck screws through the top board and into the tops of the box and divider. Next, use a circular saw or a power miter saw set at a 45° angle to bevel the front edges of the supports. Clamp the remaining top boards together, edge to edge, so the ends are flush. Center the supports on the top boards. With the beveled ends facing toward the front, drive 1⅝" deck screws through the top boards and into each support, forming the finished lid.

APPLY FINISHING TOUCHES. Cut the skids (K) to size. The skids fit below the bin to raise the box up, allowing air flow below it. Bevel both ends of each skid at 45° with a circular saw or power miter saw. Turn the bin upside down, and use wood screws to attach a skid on each side of the bin bottom, flush with the side edges. Attach the third skid at the center of the bin bottom. Use a pad sander to remove any splinters from the box. We applied a penetrating stain right after sanding, but you can let the cedar age naturally. Attach 4" strap hinges to the top of the lid, just inside the supports. Center the lid against the top of the bin, and attach the free ends of the hinges to the fixed top board **(photo D).**

Attach the shelf at the back of the box so the divider is parallel to the box sides.

Attach the lid to the top of the box with 4" strap hinges.

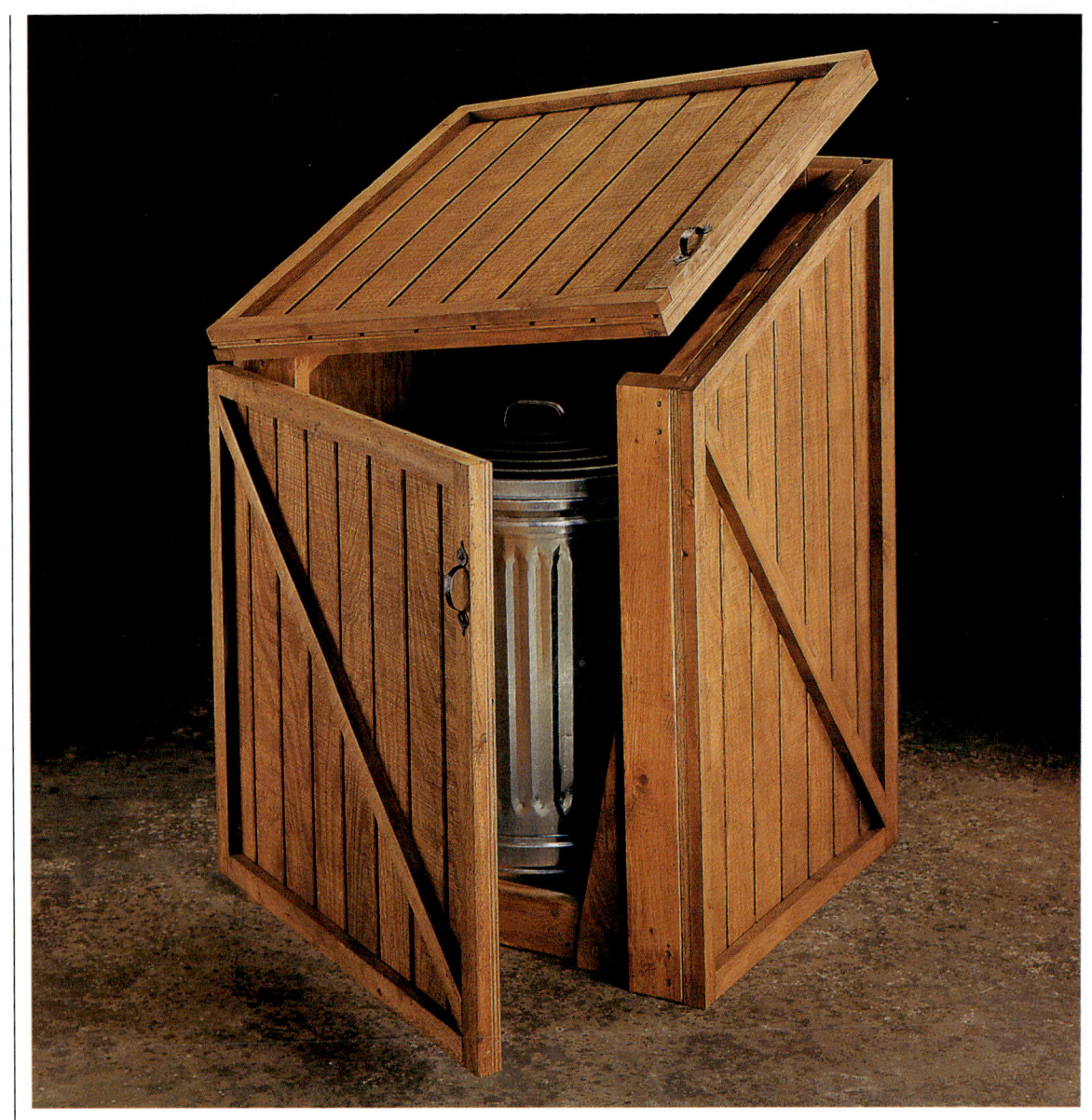

PROJECT
POWER TOOLS

Trash Can Protector

Store that unsightly garbage can in this little structure to keep it hidden and safe from pests.

CONSTRUCTION MATERIALS

Quantity	Lumber
4	2" × 4 × 8' pine
1	¾" × 2 × 4' plywood
3	⅝" × 4 × 8' grooved siding
11	1 × 2" × 8' cedar

Anyone who has spent time at a cabin or a vacation home knows that garbage can storage can be a problem. Trash cans are not only ugly, they attract raccoons and other troublesome pests. Keep the trash out of sight and away from nighttime visitors with this simple trash can protector. It accommodates a 44- gallon can and features a front and top that swing open for easy access. The 2 × 4 frame is paneled with grooved plywood siding. A cedar frame and cross rail stiffens each side panel and adds a decorative touch to the project. We used construction adhesive on this project because it adapts well to varying rates of expansion.

16 VACATION HOME FURNISHINGS

OVERALL SIZE:
48¾" HIGH
32¼" WIDE
30" DEEP

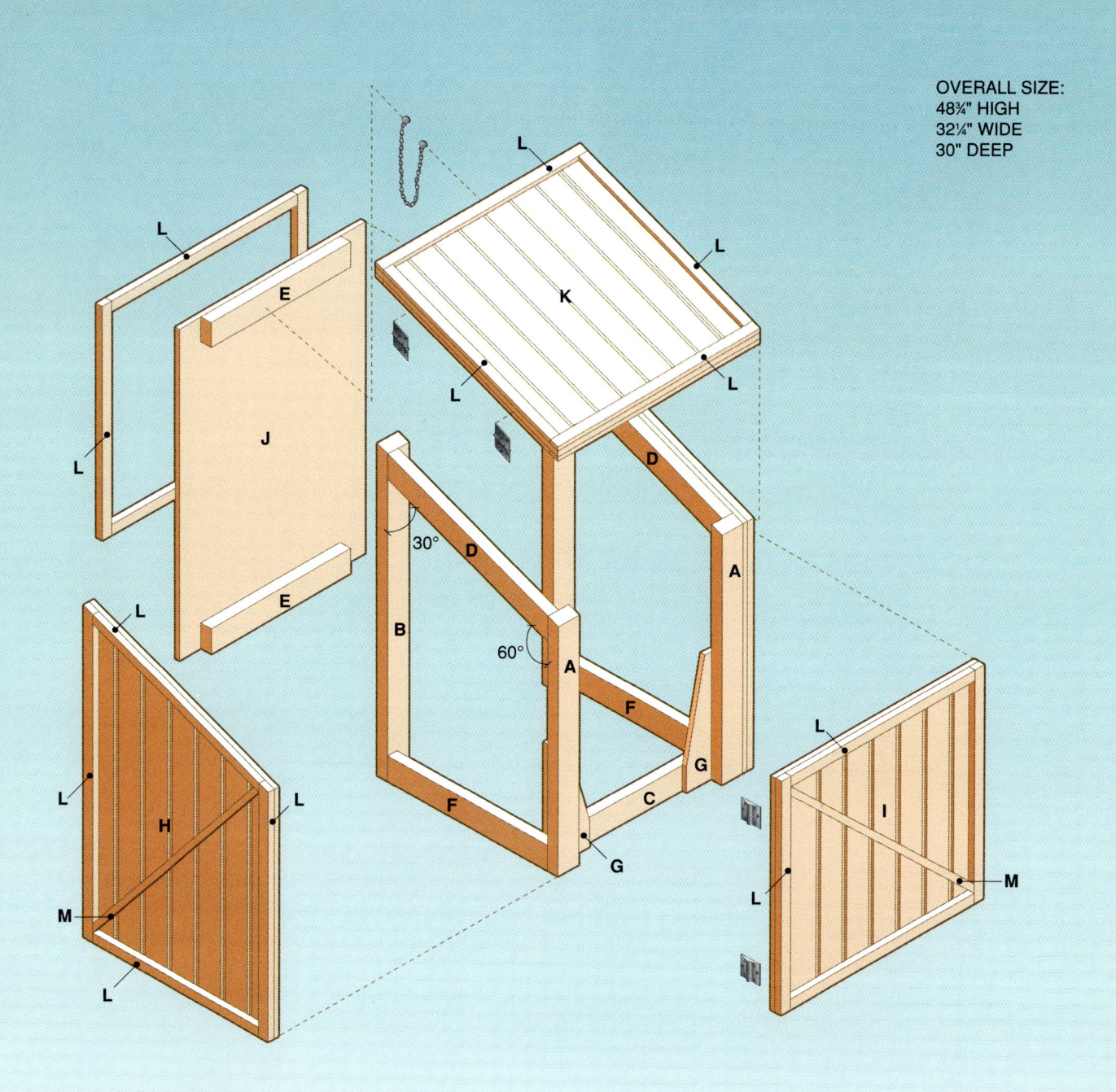

	Cutting List			
Key	Part	Dimension	Pcs.	Material
A	Front strut	1½ × 3½ × 36"	2	Pine
B	Back strut	1½ × 3½ × 46"	2	Pine
C	Front stringer	1½ × 3½ × 26¼"	1	Pine
D	Top rail	1½ × 3½ × 29¼"	2	Pine
E	Back stringer	1½ × 3½ × 22"	2	Pine
F	Bottom stringer	1½ × 3½ × 25½"	2	Pine
G	Brace	¾ × 6 × 16"	2	Plywood

	Cutting List			
Key	Part	Dimension	Pcs.	Material
H	Side panel	⅝ × 29⅛ × 45¾"	2	Plywood siding
I	Front panel	⅝ × 32¼ × 34"	1	Plywood siding
J	Back panel	⅝ × 29¼ × 45¾"	1	Plywood siding
K	Top panel	⅝ × 33¾ × 32¼"	1	Plywood siding
L	Side batten	⅞ × 1½ × *	24	Cedar
M	Cross rail	⅞ × 1½ × *	4	Cedar

Materials: Construction adhesive, deck screws (1¼", 2", 3"), 1" panhead screws (2), galvanized finish nails (6d), 3 × 3" utility hinges (2), 3 × 3" spring-loaded hinges (2), galvanized steel or plastic door pulls (2), steel chain (28"), finishing materials.

Note: Measurements reflect the actual thickness of dimensional lumber.
*Cut to fit.

VACATION HOME FURNISHINGS 17

A Make sure the back stringer is centered and flush with the bottom edge of the back before attaching it with screws and panel adhesive.

B Attach side panels to the frame, making sure the front and top edges are flush with the frame.

Directions:
Trash Can Protector

MAKE THE BACK PANEL. Start by cutting the back panel (J) to size from grooved plywood siding. Then cut the back stringers (E) to size. Position one back stringer on the ungrooved face of the back panel, flush with the bottom edge. Center the back stringer on the back panel: each end of the back stringer should be 3½" in from the back panel sides. Attach the stringer with construction adhesive and 1¼" deck screws **(photo A)**. Center the remaining back stringer on the back panel, ¾" down from the top edge, and attach it.

MAKE THE SIDE FRAMES. The sides are simple 2 × 4 frames attached to plywood panels. The frames slant downward from back to front at a 30° angle. Begin by setting a circular saw or a power miter box to cut at a 30° angle. Cut the front strut (A) and back strut (B) to length, making sure one end of each front and back strut is cut at a 30° angle. This slanted end cut should not affect the overall length of the struts (see *Diagram*, page 17). Cut the bottom stringers (F) to length. Position the front struts on edge on your worksurface. Butt the end of a bottom stringer against each front strut. The outside faces of the bottom stringers should be flush with the outside edges of the front struts, and flush with the square ends of the front struts. Apply construction adhesive, and drive 3" deck screws through the front struts and into the ends of the bottom stringers. Make sure the tops of the front struts slant in the same direction. Position a back strut against the unattached end of each bottom stringer, and attach them, making sure the slanted top ends of the back struts are facing the front struts. Next, cut the top rails (D) to length. In order for the top rails to fit between the front struts and back struts, their ends must be cut at a 60° angle. When you cut the ends, make sure they are slanted in the correct directions. (You may find it easiest to hold the top rails in place against the front and back struts, and trace the angle directly onto the top rails.) Position the top rails between the front struts and back struts, making sure the outside faces are flush with the outside edges of the front struts and back struts. Attach the top rails with construction adhesive and 3" deck screws.

MAKE & ATTACH THE SIDE BRACES. The braces strengthen the frame and fit just behind the front struts, flush with the bottom stringers. Cut the braces (G) to size. Cut a slanted profile on the braces, so the top edge is 3" long and the bottom edge is 6" long. This slanted profile leaves room to move a garbage can in and out of the unit. Position the braces against the inside faces of the front struts, making sure the braces butt against the bottom stringers. Fasten the braces with construction adhesive and 2" deck screws.

JOIN THE SIDES. The two side frames are now joined to create a rough box frame. Start by cutting the front stringer (C) to length. Stand the side frames up on your worksurface so the front struts face the same direc-

18 VACATION HOME FURNISHINGS

Mark the ends of the cross rails before cutting them to fit between the frame corners.

tion. Position the front stringer between the side frames with one face butting against each brace. Make sure the ends of the front stringer are in contact with the bottom stringers, and attach the front stringer with construction adhesive and 3" deck screws.

COMPLETE THE FRAME. Position the back panel against the frame sides. Make sure the back stringers are flush against the back struts, and attach the back panel to the frame with construction adhesive and 1¼" deck screws. The side edges of the back should be flush with the frame sides. Cut the side panels (H) to the size shown in the *Cutting List*. Set the side panels against the frame sides, making sure the front and rear edges align and the panel is resting squarely on the ground. Trace the top edge of the frame onto the back (ungrooved) face of the side panels. Cut along the line with a circular saw. Attach the side panels with construction adhesive and screws **(photo B)**.

ATTACH THE BATTENS & CROSS RAILS. The battens are pieces of trim that frame the panels along their edges. The cross rails fit diagonally from corner to corner on the side panels. Measure the sides carefully before cutting the battens to length. Cut the battens (L) to fit along the side and back panel edges. Once the battens have been cut to length, fasten them to the side panels with construction adhesive and 6d finish nails. Position the diagonal side battens on the sides so they span from corner to corner. Mark the angle required for the ends to fit snugly into the corners **(photo C)**. Cut the cross rails to size and attach them. The back battens form a simple frame around the back. Attach the back battens, making sure their outside and top edges are flush with the side faces and top edges of the rear side battens.

MAKE THE TOP & FRONT PANELS. The top and front panels are framed in the same way as the side panels and back panels. Start by cutting the top panel (K) and front panel (I) to size from grooved plywood siding. Cut these parts from the same sheet of siding to make sure the grooves align on the finished project. Cut battens to frame the edges of the top panel on both faces, then attach battens on the front panel. Like the side panels, the front panel is framed on one face only, and has a cross rail stretching from corner to corner. Attach two spring-loaded, self-closing hinges to the front panel, and mount it on the front of the project. The bottom edge of the front panel should be 1" up from the bottoms of the stringers. Mount the top panel with two 3×3" utility hinges **(photo D).** Attach handles or pulls on the front and top of the garbage can holder. Use two panhead screws to attach a 28"-long safety chain to the back edge of the back stringer and top panel to keep the top panel from swinging open too far. Fasten the ends of the chain 10" in from the hinged edge of the top panel. Finish the trash can protector with an exterior-rated stain. If pests are a serious problem, attach latches to the front and top to hold them in place.

Mount the top to the top of a side panel with 3×3" utility hinges.

VACATION HOME FURNISHINGS 19

PROJECT
POWER TOOLS

Modular Couch

Support cubes, a platform bench and removable backrests can be combined to meet a variety of seating and storage needs.

It's a couch…it's a sun lounger…it's a pair of matching chairs or end tables…indoors or outdoors, this Swiss army knife of cabin furnishings is virtually unlimited in the seating options it offers.

Two square cubes form the base for this modular couch. Simply set the bench platform on top of the cubes and insert the three backrests into the slots, and you have a spacious couch that seats three comfortably (especially if you add a few throw pillows). Or, insert a backrest directly into each cube to form matching chairs (or leave the backrests out and use the cubes as matching end tables). For an added bonus, remove the cube tops to gain access to two generous storage compartments.

The bench itself is lightweight and portable—perfect for hauling out to the deck or patio for a bit of sunbathing. Or, remove the backrests, lay a foam cushion on the bench, and you're set with an emergency guest bed.

Solid, simple components make this modular couch the perfect workhorse for any home where seating needs can be unpredictable.

Construction Materials

Quantity	Lumber
7	1 × 4" × 8' pine
15	1 × 6" × 8' pine
7	2 × 4" × 8' pine

OVERALL SIZE:
35" HIGH
27½" DEEP
84½" LONG

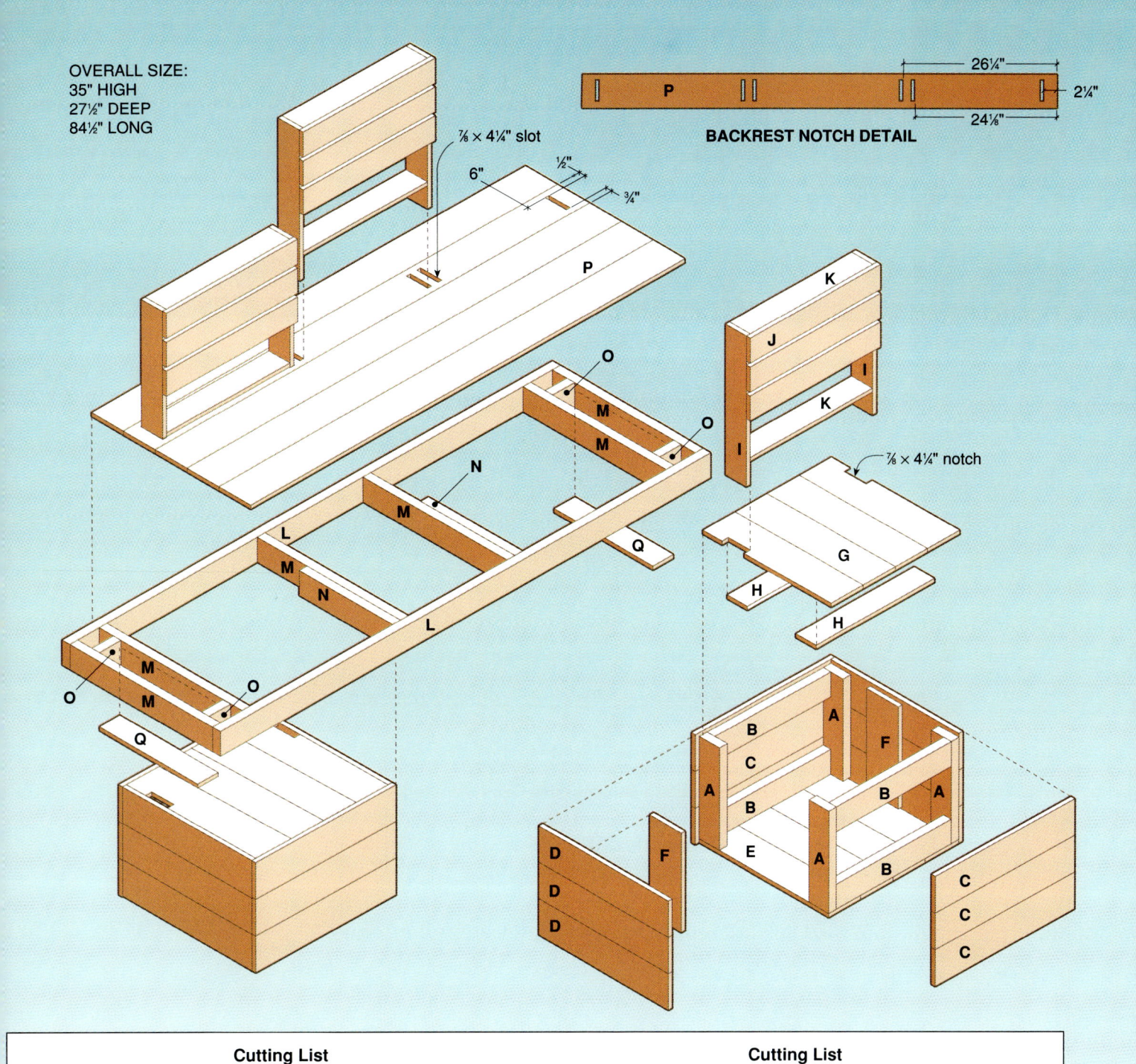

⅞ × 4¼" slot

6"
½"
¾"

26¼"
2¼"
24⅛"

BACKREST NOTCH DETAIL

⅞ × 4¼" notch

Key	Part	Cutting List Dimension	Pcs.	Material
A	Cube frame	1½ × 3½ × 15"	8	Pine
B	Cube frame	1½ × 3½ × 19½"	8	Pine
C	Cube side	¾ × 5½ × 24"	12	Pine
D	Cube side	¾ × 5½ × 22½"	12	Pine
E	Cube bottom	¾ × 5½ × 22½"	8	Pine
F	Cube cleat	¾ × 5½ × 15"	4	Pine
G	Cube top	¾ × 5½ × 22"	8	Pine
H	Cube stringer	¾ × 3½ × 19⅜"	4	Pine
I	Backrest stile	¾ × 3½ × 22¾"	6	Pine

Key	Part	Cutting List Dimension	Pcs.	Material
J	Backrest slat	¾ × 3½ × 22½"	9	Pine
K	Backrest slat	¾ × 3½ × 21"	6	Pine
L	Bench rail	1½ × 3½ × 84½"	2	Pine
M	Bench crossrail	1½ × 3½ × 24½"	6	Pine
N	Bench block	1½ × 3½ × 16¼"	2	Pine
O	Bench spacer	1½ × 3½ × 3½"	4	Pine
P	Bench slat	¾ × 5½ × 74½"	5	Pine
Q	Cup holder	¾ × 3½ × 18"	2	Pine

Materials: Wood glue, deck screws (1", 2", 2½"), finishing materials.
Note: Measurements reflect the actual thickness of dimensional lumber.

VACATION HOME FURNISHINGS 21

A

Attach the cube side boards to the cube frames, checking to make sure the corners are square as you work.

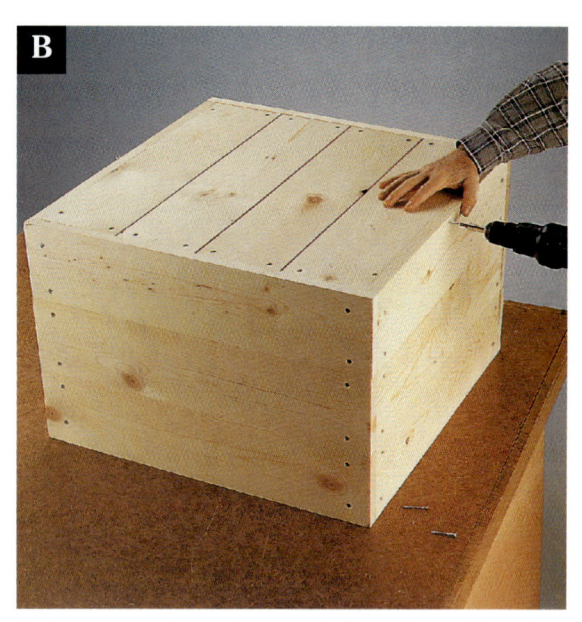

B

Drive screws through the side boards and into the edges of the bottom boards to strengthen the cube.

Directions:
Modular Couch

MAKE THE CUBE FRAMES. The cubes provide support for the bench and backrests. They are simple 2 × 6 frames clad with 1 × 6 pine. The removable top panels are notched to accept the backrest stiles. The number of pieces shown in the *Cutting List* on page 21 is sufficient to build two cubes. Start by cutting the cube frames (A, B) to size. The longer frame pieces (B) are horizontal rails that fit between the shorter pieces (A), which are vertical stiles. Each cube frame is made up of two sets of four pieces that are joined together by the cube boards. Apply glue to the ends of the longer cube frame boards, and sandwich them in pairs between the vertical pieces, flush with the bottoms and tops. Drive 2½" deck screws through the vertical pieces and into the ends of the horizontal pieces to create four frame sets. Cut the cube bottom (E) boards to length and lay them edge to edge in sets of four, making sure the ends are flush. Set a cube frame assembly at each end of each set so the ends are flush, and attach the frames to the bottom boards with glue and 2½" deck screws driven up through the bottom boards and into the frames.

ATTACH THE CUBE SIDES. The cube side boards are fastened around the cube frames to create an open-topped box, which is reinforced on the inner walls by 1 × 6 cleats. Cut the cube sides (C, D) and cube cleats (F) to length. Starting at the bottom of one cube frame, attach the shorter side boards (D) to the outside faces of the vertical cube frame pieces (A), using glue and deck screws. The ends of the side boards should be flush with the outer edges of the vertical cube frame pieces. As you attach each cube side board, check to make sure the corners of the cube are square **(photo A).** When you're finished attaching the shorter side boards on both ends of each cube, the tops of the vertical frame pieces should be ¾" down from the top edges of the upper side boards. Next, use glue and wood screws to attach the longer side boards (C). The ends of the longer side boards should be flush with the outer faces of the shorter side boards, and the seams between boards should be aligned on all sides. Then, with the cube upside down, drive countersunk 2" deck screws through the side boards and into the bottom boards to strengthen the cube **(photo B).** Finally, position cube cleats inside each cube, running vertically, 3½" in from the one cube frame assembly—use a 1 × 4 spacer to set the correct distance **(photo C).** Fasten the cube cleats with glue and 1¼" deck screws, driven though the cleats and into the side boards.

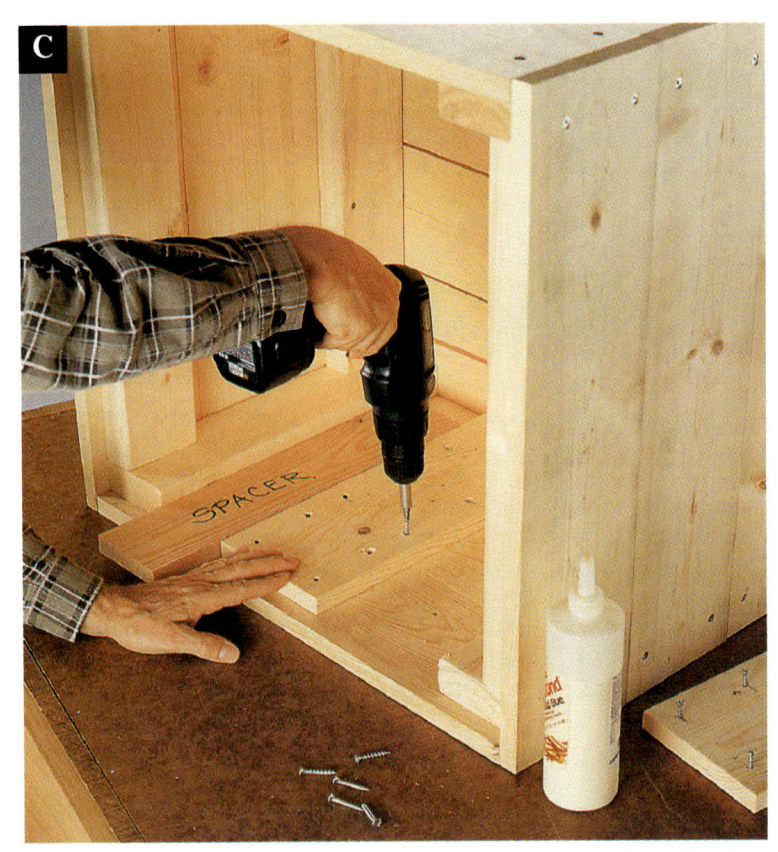

Use a spacer to maintain the correct distance between the cube cleat and the cube frame. Fasten it with glue and screws.

MAKE THE CUBE TOPS. The cube tops are built to fit into the open ends of the cubes. They feature notched handholds so the tops can be lifted off easily to access the storage compartment inside each cube. Cut the cube top boards (G) and cube stringers (H) to length. Arrange the top boards edge to edge in groups of four, with their ends flush. Draw reference lines across the top boards, 1⅜" in from each end. Position a stringer on each reference line so the outside edges are flush with the line. There should be a 1¼"-wide gap from the ends of the stringers to the edges of the top boards. Attach the stringers with glue and countersunk 1¼" deck screws, driven through the stretchers and into the top boards. Each outside top board has a ⅞"-deep × 4¼"-long rectangular notch cut into its outside edge. The notches start 3¼" in from one end of the top boards (see *Diagram*). Draw the cutting lines, and cut the notches with a jig saw **(photo D)**.

BUILD THE BACKRESTS. The backrests fit into the handholds in the cubes to form chairs. Later in the construction process, notches are made in the bench seat for the backrests, forming a comfortable modular couch. Start by cutting the backrest stiles (I) and backrest slats (J, K) to length. Position two stiles on edge so their ends are flush. Draw reference lines across one long edge of each stile, 4¼" up from one end (this end will be the bottom). Also draw reference lines 4½" and 9" down from the top ends of the stiles. Apply glue to the ends of the shorter slats (K), and fit them on edge between the stiles. One slat should be flush with the top ends of the stiles; position the other short slat so its bottom face is on the 4¼" reference line. Check to make sure the parts are square, and drive 2" deck screws through the stiles and into the ends of the slats. Use glue and deck screws to fasten one of the longer slats (K) to the stiles, flush with the top ends. Attach the remaining long slats with their top edges on the 4½" and 9" reference lines. Round over the edges of the backrests with a power sander **(photo E)** or with a router and ¼" roundover bit.

MAKE THE BENCH FRAME. The bench section is a platform that fits over the cubes to form the couch. The bench frame is made by attaching crossrails between a long pair of rails. After support pieces (spacers and blocks) are inserted into the frame, a cup holder board is inserted at each end of the frame—on the completed project there is a recessed area at each end of the seat for holding glasses, cups and cans. Finally, slats are attached to

TIP

When applying a finish to fresh wood, always treat both faces of the board the same way. For example, applying paint to only one of the wood surfaces can cause the boards to warp—especially if you use the furnishing outdoors or in areas with high moisture levels. For this reason, it is often easier to paint the project parts while you can still access them, before assembly of the project is completed.

VACATION HOME FURNISHINGS 23

Use a jig saw to cut the notches for the backrest stiles on each side of the cube top, then sand or file the notches smooth.

Smooth the sharp edges of the backrest with a power sander or a router and roundover bit.

complete the couch seat. Begin by cutting the bench rails (L) and bench crossrails (M) to size. After sanding the parts, position the bench rails together on edge with their ends flush. Draw reference lines across the top edges 5" and 32½" in from each end. Set the two bench rails about 24½" apart on your worksurface. Position a crossrail on edge between the bench rails, flush with the ends. Fasten it with glue and countersunk 2½" deck screws. Continue attaching the crossrails, working your way from one end of the bench rails to the other **(photo F),** and keeping the outside faces of the crossrails flush with the reference lines. Use a framing square to check for square as you go.

COMPLETE THE BENCH. Cut the bench blocks (N), bench spacers (O) and cup holders (Q) to size. Sand all the parts after cutting, and round the edges of the cup holders. Designate a front and rear edge of the bench frame. Use glue and 2½" deck screws to fasten a bench block to the outside face of each inner crossrail so one end of each bench block butts against the front bench rail. Position two spacers between the outside crossrails at each end of the bench frame (the outside faces of the spacers should be 2" in from the bench rails). Fasten the spacers with glue and deck screws. Center the cup holders in the gap between the spacers, leaving a ¼"-wide gap between the ends of the cup holders and the spacers. Position a 1¼"-thick spacer underneath each cup holder, and fasten the cup

Starting at one end of the bench rails, attach the crossrails at the reference lines, making sure to check for square as you go.

24 VACATION HOME FURNISHINGS

holders with glue and 2½" deck screws **(photo G).** Cut the bench slats (P), and sand them to smooth out any rough edges. Position the slats one by one over the bench frame so the ends of the slats are flush with the first inner crossrails. Mark the positions of the crossrails on the slats to help you align pilot-hole centerpoints. Fasten the rear bench slat to the crossrails with glue and countersunk 2" deck screws. Set the next bench slat in place, but do not fasten it. Position the remaining bench slats in place, and attach them with glue and 2" deck screws. Remove the loose slat. This slat must be cut with notches to hold the backrests in place. To mark the cutting lines for the ⅞"-wide × 3¾"-long notches, see the *Diagram*, page 21. Drill ⅜"-dia. starter holes inside the cutting lines **(photo H),** and cut the notches with a jig saw. Smooth out the insides of the notches with a file or sander. Position the notched slat onto the bench frame, and fasten it with glue and countersunk wood screws.

APPLY FINISHING TOUCHES. Fill all countersunk screw holes with wood putty. Sand all wood surfaces with medium-grit sandpaper to smooth out any rough spots. Prime and paint the project inside and out. Because there is considerable contact between components as the modular couch is assembled and disassembled, be sure to use a high-quality enamel paint (exterior-rated is preferable) to paint the components.

OPTIONS FOR ARRANGING YOUR MODULAR COUCH. The introduction to this article (page 20) describes the basic ways that the modular couch can be put together to fulfill multiple seating needs. The basic arrangements are the couch, matching chairs, matching end tables, sun lounger and guest bed. As you use the modular couch system, you will likely discover new ways that the parts can be used together. By building two modular couches, you can expand your options still further to include such furnishings as a double guest bed and a sectional sofa arrangement.

Fasten the cup holders between the outside crossrails, making sure they are centered front to back.

With the cutting lines for the notches drawn, drill a starter hole, and cut the notches with a jig saw.

VACATION HOME FURNISHINGS 25

Cottage Clock

This cottage clock uses wood appliqués to reproduce an early 19th century clock design.

PROJECT POWER TOOLS

This reproduction of a "cottage clock" style mantel clock is modeled after a design by Eli Terry from 1816. The mantel clock emerged as a mainstay of the American home back in Colonial times. Although the first models customarily were set on the fireplace mantel, the basic design has evolved to include many types of small clocks that can be positioned anywhere in your home. The primary feature that most mantel clocks share is their size—large enough to be noticed, but smaller than an upright floor clock. Many mantel clocks, including the "cottage clock" design shown here, have a door or false door on the front of the clock cabinet. The doors usually have an upper panel that contains the clock face, and a decorative lower panel (lower panels frequently are made of glass to reveal the pendulum on mechanical clocks).

Making the cabinet for this cottage clock is a simple, inexpensive project that can easily be accomplished in a single afternoon. We used ½"-thick clear pine to build the cabinet frame (most clocks of this type were made with pine, frequently with a hardwood veneer layer). The decorative elements are created with milled moldings and appliqués. The clock itself is an inexpensive battery-operated model. Most woodworker's stores and craft stores carry a wide selection of clocks.

Construction Materials

Quantity	Lumber
1	½ × 6" × 4' pine
1	¾ × 3½" × 4' pine
1	⅛ × ¾" × 5' pine shelf nosing
1	½ × 2¼" × 3' pine casing
1	½ × 1⅛" × 3' cap molding

26 VACATION HOME FURNISHINGS

OVERALL SIZE:
13" HIGH
4" DEEP
7¾" WIDE

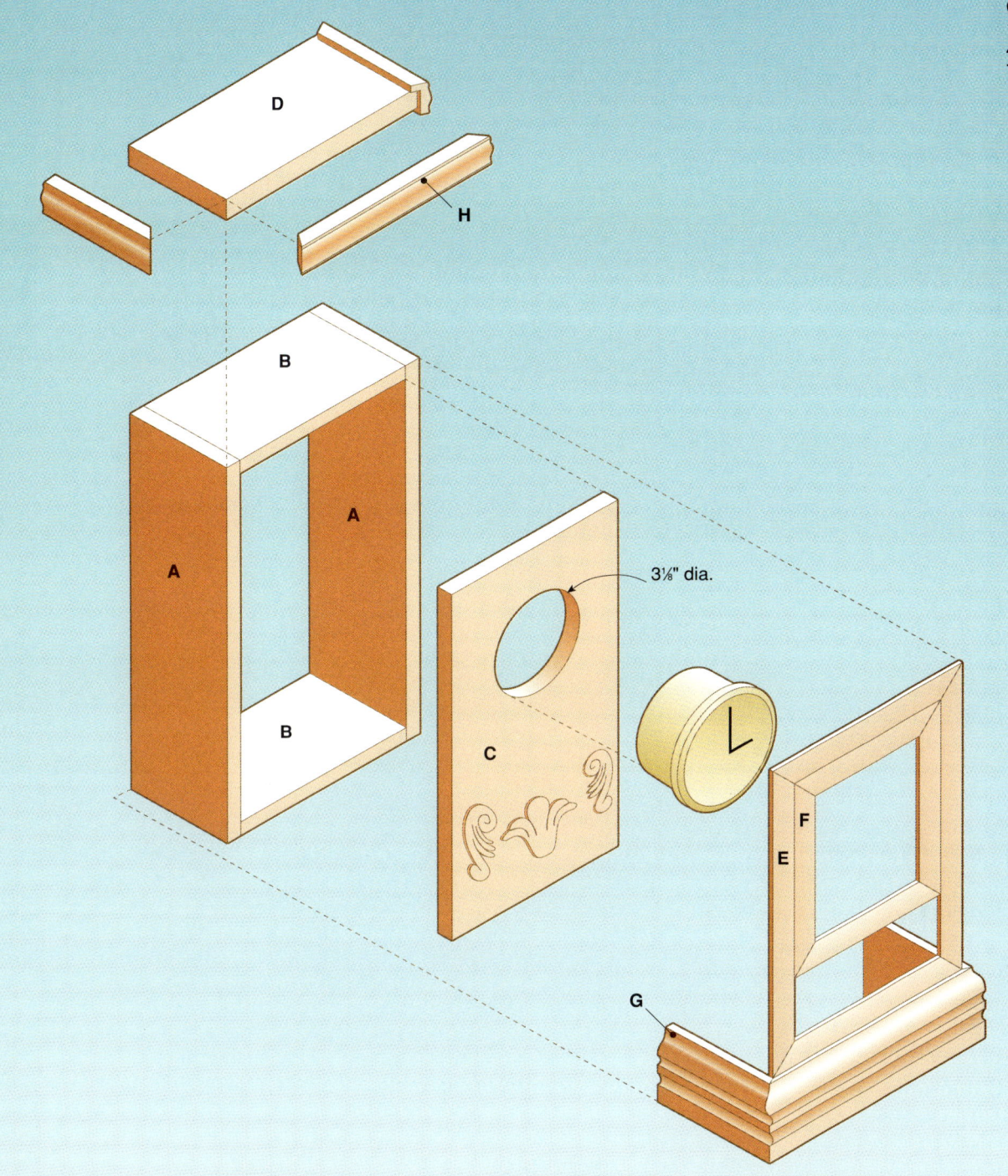

Cutting List

Key	Part	Dimension	Pcs.	Material
A	Side	½ × 3½ × 12"	2	Pine
B	End	½ × 3½ × 6"	2	Pine
C	Face board	½ × 6 × 11"	1	Pine
D	Crown board	¾ × 3½ × 7"	1	Pine

Cutting List

Key	Part	Dimension	Pcs.	Material
E	Outside trim	⅛ × ¾" × *	4	Shelf nosing
F	Inside trim	⅛ × ¾" × *	4	Shelf nosing
G	Base molding	½ × 2¼" × *	3	Pine casing
H	Crown piece	½ × 1⅛" × *	3	Cap molding

Materials: Glue, 1" wire brads, 3⅛"-dia. battery-powered clock, decorative wood carvings, finishing materials.
Note: Measurements reflect the actual thickness of dimensional lumber.
* Cut to fit

VACATION HOME FURNISHINGS 27

Directions: Cottage Clock

MAKE THE FACE BOARD. This cottage clock cabinet is essentially a pine frame with a cover and a few decorative accents. The battery-operated clock fits into a hole in the front of the cabinet cover—called the face board. Cut the face board (C) to size from ½"-thick pine (most building centers carry ½"-thick solid boards in varying widths and lengths with their shelving and craft products). The size of the cutout for the clock should be based on the diameter of your clock back. The clock we installed has a 3⅛" back diameter. To make the cutout for the clock, add 1½" to the *radius* (½ the diameter) of the clock back, measure down that amount from the top of the face board, and draw a reference line. Next, measure in 3" from one side of the face board and mark a point on the reference line to find the centerpoint for the cutout. Set a compass to the radius of the clock back (in our case, 1 9/16"). Drill a starter hole inside the circle, and make the cutout with a jig saw. Because the flange of the clock face will cover the edges of the hole, it's okay if the cut is a little rough.

MAKE THE CABINET. The clock cabinet frames the face board. Begin by cutting the sides (A) and ends (B) to length from 3½"-wide ½"-thick pine. Fasten the sides and ends into a frame, using the face board as a guide. The cabinet sides should overlap the cabinet ends. Make the joints with glue and 1" wire brads, driven through the sides and into the ends. Remove the face board from the frame, and apply glue to the edges. Reinsert it into the frame so the front face is flush with the front edges of the cabinet frame. Drive a few 1" wire brads through the frame and into the edges of the face board **(photo A)**. Although pine is a soft wood, it is a good idea to drill tiny pilot holes for the brads before you drive them. Use a pad sander with fine (about 150-grit) sandpaper to even out all the joints, as

Use the face board as a guide when nailing together the corners of the cabinet frame.

Attach strips of miter-cut cap molding to the front and sides of the crown board, then attach the assembly to the top of the cabinet.

TIP

Decorative wood carvings, sold at most woodworker's or craft stores, are generally made from oak or birch, but they will blend in with pine, especially if a darker stain is used. When selecting any appliqués (carvings or otherwise), bring a template of the project with you to the store so you can test out different shapes and combinations.

28 VACATION HOME FURNISHINGS

well as smooth out the surfaces of the cabinet.

ATTACH THE CROWN. The crown is the decorative top on the clock cabinet. It is made by framing a piece of ¾"-thick pine with three pieces of ½"-thick × 1⅛"-wide cap molding. Cut the crown board (D) to length, and sand the edges smooth. Then, miter-cut the cap molding into three crown pieces (H) that frame the front and side of the crown board—start by cutting the front strip with 45° ends, then cut the side strips to fit. The back ends of the side strips should be square-cut. Apply glue to the crown pieces, then attach them to the crown board with 1" wire nails. Then, fasten the crown assembly to the top of the cabinet, making sure the back edges are flush and the overhang is equal on both sides, using glue and 1" wire nails **(photo B)**.

ATTACH THE BASE MOLDING. The base molding is made and installed exactly like the pieces of cap molding that frame the crown board. Instead of cap molding, however, use ½ × 2¼" case molding (case molding with decorative contours is a good choice). Cut the base molding pieces (G) to fit around the front and sides of the frame and form clean mitered corners. Attach them, then finish-sand the cabinet.

FRAME THE FACE BOARD. We added decorative trim (⅛ × ¾" shelf nosing) to the clock to create a false door frame that is glued to the face board. A second frame inside the first divides the false door into upper and lower panels. Cut the outside trim pieces (E) to fit around the perimeter of the face board, miter-cutting the

Use ⅛ × ¾" shelf nosing to make frames on the face board, creating the illusion of a cabinet door with upper and lower panels.

For a decorative touch, we glued a set of milled wood carvings (two small seraphs and a tulip design) to the lower panel of the face board.

corners. Using glue only, attach the outside trim **(photo C)**. Then, cut the inside trim (F) to make the internal frame. Check to make sure the clock cutout is centered within the internal frame, then attach the inside trim. Rest a book on the trim frames while the glue dries.

DECORATE THE LOWER PANEL. Glue milled wooden carvings (or add another decorative element, such as stencils) to the lower panel for a nice decorative touch **(photo D)**.

APPLY FINISHING TOUCHES. Fill any exposed holes with untinted wood putty. Sand the surfaces, and apply your finish of choice (we used walnut stain with a tung-oil topcoat). Install the clock according to the manufacturer's directions. OPTION: If the back of the clock will be visible, cut a back panel to fit inside the frame, using ½"-thick pine. Sand and finish the back of the clock.

VACATION HOME FURNISHINGS 29

PROJECT
POWER TOOLS

Cedar Bench

The rugged simplicity of this cedar bench is well suited for any cabin or cottage setting.

Construction Materials	
Quantity	**Lumber**
3	1 × 4" × 8' cedar
2	2 × 10" × 6' cedar
1	2 × 4" × 8' cedar

This slender cedar bench has remarkably clean lines and a nice appearance, which makes it look great anywhere you put it—on a deck, in a cabin or by a backyard fire pit. A full 5 feet in length, it can seat up to three adults comfortably. Or if you prefer, it can be surrounded with other chairs or benches to do double duty as a cocktail or coffee table.

Although this cedar bench is lightweight and very simple to build, it can withstand heavy use and exposure to sun and rain. And because the construction is so simple, you can easily shorten the length to fit a special spot by shortening the 2 × 10 seat planks and the side aprons. Or, take it one step further and build the bench to a square shape for use as a one-person seat or an end table.

30 VACATION HOME FURNISHINGS

OVERALL SIZE:
17" HIGH
20¼" DEEP
61¾" LONG

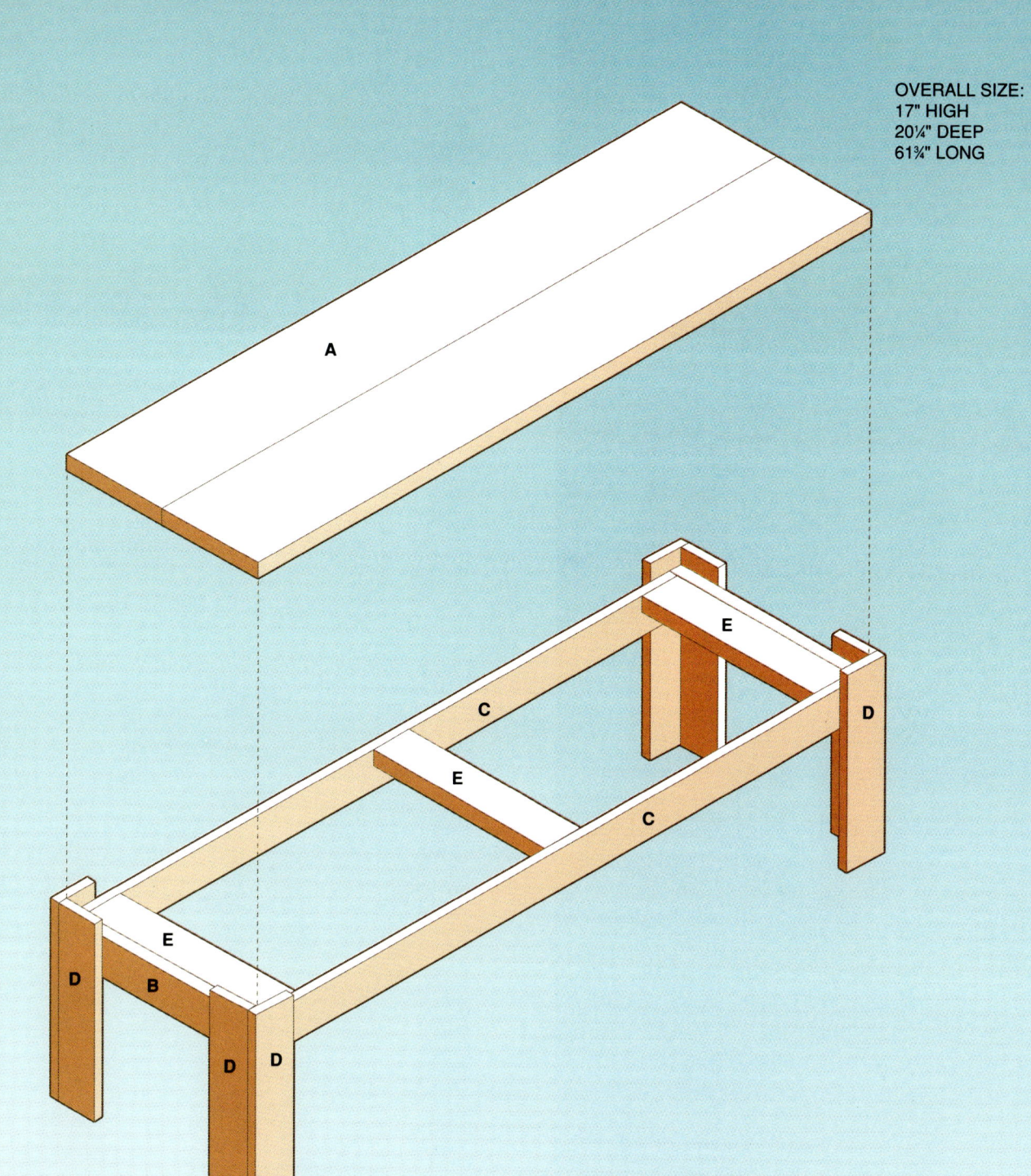

Cutting List					Cutting List			
Key	Part	Dimension	Pcs.	Material	Key	Part	Dimension	Pcs.	Material
A	Seat slat	1½ × 9¼ × 60"	2	Cedar	D	Leg board	⅞ × 3½ × 17"	8	Cedar
B	End apron	1½ × 3½ × 18½"	2	Cedar	E	Cleat	1½ × 3½ × 16¾"	3	Cedar
C	Side apron	⅞ × 3½ × 57"	2	Cedar					

Materials: Moisture-resistant wood glue, deck screws (2", 2½"), ⅜"-dia. cedar plugs, finishing materials.

Note: Measurements reflect the actual thickness of dimensional lumber.

VACATION HOME FURNISHINGS 31

A

The legs are made by joining pairs of 1 × 4s at right angles.

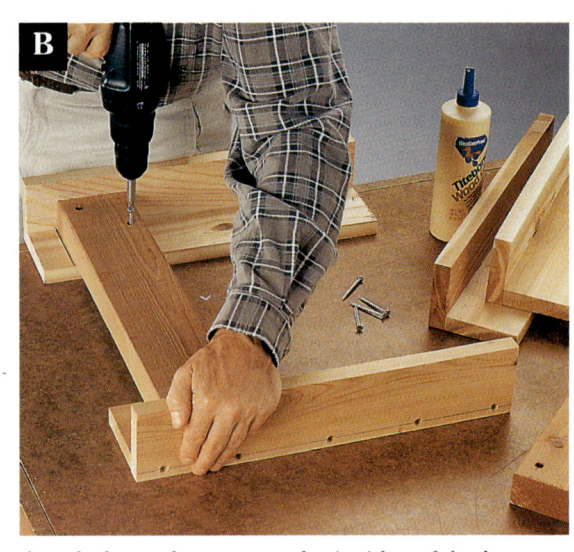

B

Attach the end aprons to the insides of the leg pairs, 1½" down from the tops of the legs.

Directions: Cedar Bench

MAKE THE LEGS. Each leg is made by fastening the edges of two pieces of 1 × 4 cedar together at a right angle to create an L-shape. Begin by cutting the leg boards (D) to size, and sand them to smooth out any rough edges. Butt a long edge of one leg board against a face of another leg board—since most dimensional cedar lumber is smoother on one face, be careful to keep faces of similar smoothness exposed. Join the leg-board pairs together into legs, using moisture-resistant wood glue and 2" deck screws driven through pilot holes. Be sure to counterbore the pilot holes deep enough to accept a ⅜"-dia. cedar plug (if you are not overly concerned about creating a clean, finished appearance, go ahead and drive the deck screws into pilot holes that are only countersunk slightly—just make sure the screw heads are recessed below the surface of the wood). Continue assembling the leg-board pairs until all four legs are complete **(photo A)**.

ATTACH THE END APRONS. The end aprons fit between the legs at the ends of the bench. Unlike standard aprons, they are attached to the inside faces of the legs, which gives them a cleaner appearance and allows them to provide greater structural support. To minimize the number of exposed screw heads in the legs, we attached the end aprons and side aprons by driving screws through the aprons and into the legs—this can be a little tricky because you have to be very careful how far you countersink or counterbore the pilot holes to keep the screw tips from protruding out through the faces of the legs. If you are not troubled by exposed screw heads, or

C

Fasten the side aprons to the insides of the legs so they are flush with the end aprons.

32 VACATION HOME FURNISHINGS

Fasten 1 × 4 cleats to the undersides of the seat slats to tie them together and help prevent sagging.

After the seat boards are cleated together, set them on the aprons and secure them with deck screws.

ATTACH THE SIDE APRONS. The 1 × 4 side aprons connect the leg/end apron assemblies. Like the end aprons, the side aprons support the seat slats on the completed bench. Cut the side aprons (C) to length. Set the leg assemblies on a flat worksurface, 57" apart. Apply glue to the ends of the side aprons, and position them between the legs, flush with the tops of the end aprons. Drive countersunk 1⅝" deck screws through the end aprons and into the legs **(photo C)**.

MAKE THE SEAT. The seat for the cedar bench is simply a pair of 2 × 10s laid together edge to edge. Three cleats are attached beneath the seat slats to tie them together and help prevent sagging. Cut the seat slats (A) and cleats (E) to size. Clamp the seat slats together, edge to edge, making sure the ends are flush. Draw a reference line 1½" in from each end to mark position for the outer cleats. Set a cleat against each line, then set another in between the outer cleats. Drill pilot holes, and attach the cleats with glue and 2½" deck screws **(photo D)**. Stand the leg assembly upright. Set the seat into the recess created by the tops of the aprons, and fasten it by driving 1⅝" deck screws through the aprons and into the cleats **(photo E)**.

APPLY FINISHING TOUCHES. Glue ⅜"-dia. cedar wood plugs into all the counterbores in the exposed faces of the legs and aprons, then sand the plugs even with the wood after the glue dries. Finish-sand the wood surfaces, then apply your finish of choice—we used a tinted exterior wood stain.

don't mind counterboring and plugging additional holes in the legs, then you may want to screw through the legs and into the aprons. Cut the end aprons (B) to length. Sand the ends, and set two leg pairs on your worksurface, about 21" apart. Position an end apron between the leg boards so the top edge of the apron is 1½" down from the tops of the legs. Drill countersunk pilot holes, and attach the ends with glue and 2" deck screws, driven through the ends and into the legs **(photo B)**. Use plenty of moisture-resistant wood glue to reinforce the joint, and drive at least two screws into each leg board. Attach both end aprons between pairs of legs.

VACATION HOME FURNISHINGS 33

PROJECT
POWER TOOLS

Dock Box

This spacious dockside hold protects all your boating supplies, with room to spare.

Construction Materials	
Quantity	**Lumber**
2	⅝" × 4 × 8' plywood siding
7	1 × 2" × 8' cedar
4	1 × 4" × 8' cedar
1	1 × 6" × 8' cedar
3	2 × 2" × 8' cedar

With a spacious storage compartment and an appealing nautical design, this dock box is a perfect place for stowing water sports equipment so you don't have to haul it inside after every offshore excursion. Life preservers, beach toys, ropes and even small coolers conveniently fit inside this attractive chest, which has ventilation holes to discourage mildew. Sturdy enough for seating, the large top can hold charts, fishing gear or a light snack while you await the next trip out.

With a dock box to hold your gear, you can spend your energy carrying more important items, like the fresh catch of the day, up to your cabin.

34 VACATION HOME FURNISHINGS

OVERALL SIZE:
30" HIGH
49¾" LONG
23¾" DEEP

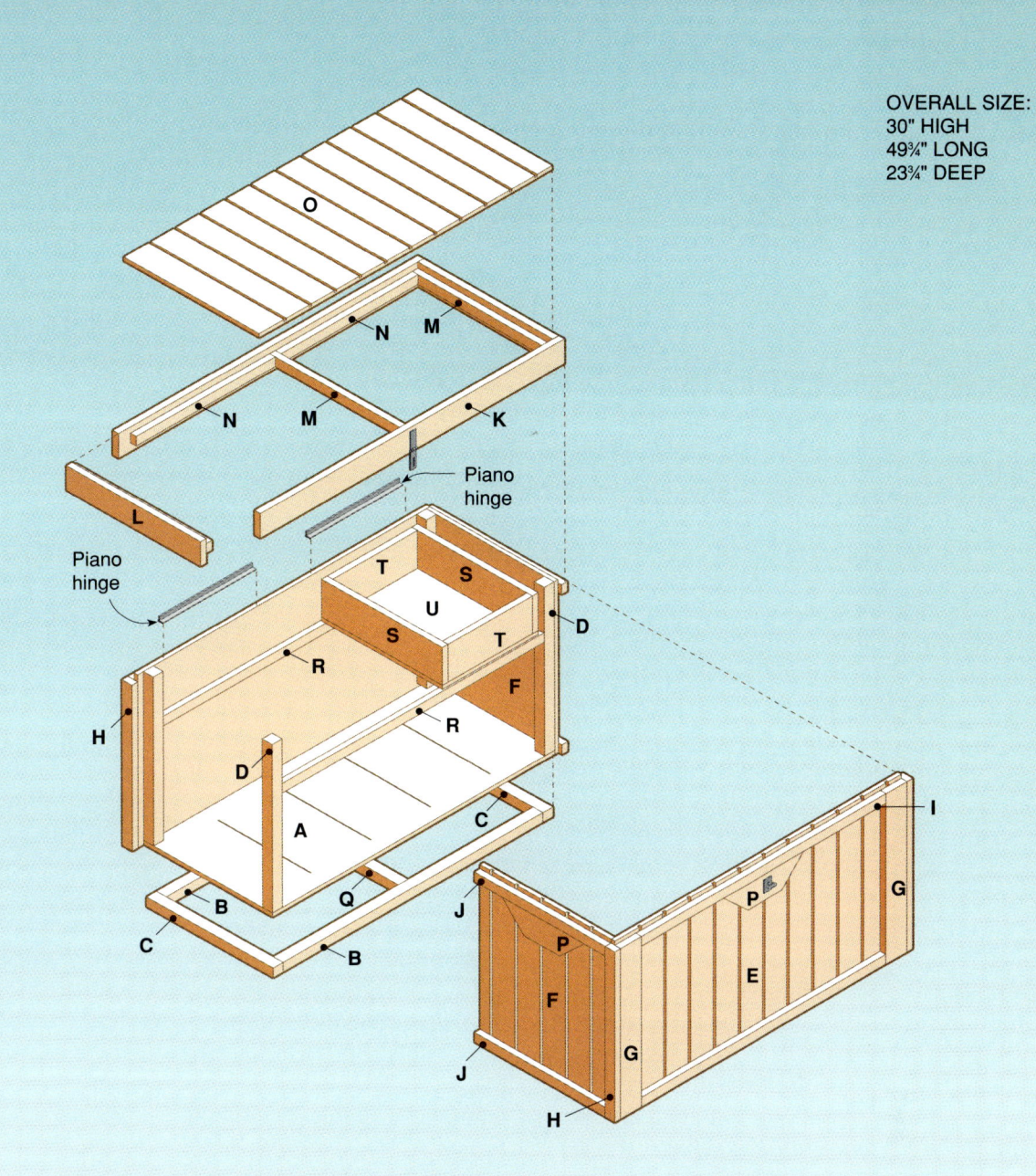

Cutting List					Cutting List				
Key	Part	Dimension	Pcs.	Material	Key	Part	Dimension	Pcs.	Material
A	Bottom	⅝ × 20½ × 46¼"	1	Pine plywood	L	Lid end	⅞ × 3½ × 21⅝"	2	Cedar
B	Bottom brace	1½ × 1½ × 43¼"	2	Cedar	M	Top support	⅞ × 1½ × 21⅝"	3	Cedar
C	Brace end	1½ × 1½ × 20½"	2	Cedar	N	Ledger	⅞ × 1½ × 22¾"	4	Cedar
D	Corner brace	1½ × 1½ × 24⅜"	4	Cedar	O	Top panel	⅝ × 21⅝ × 48"	1	Pine plywood
E	Large panel	⅝ × 27 × 47½"	2	Pine plywood	P	Handle	⅞ × 3½ × 13½"	4	Cedar
F	Small panel	⅝ × 27 × 20½"	2	Pine plywood	Q	Cross brace	1½ × 1½ × 17½	1	Cedar
G	Corner trim	⅞ × 3½ × 26½"	4	Cedar	R	Tray slide	⅞ × 1½ × 43¼"	2	Cedar
H	Corner batten	⅞ × 1½ × 26½"	4	Cedar	S	Tray side	⅞ × 5½ × 20½"	2	Cedar
I	Long trim	⅞ × 1½ × 42¼"	4	Cedar	T	Tray end	⅞ × 5½ × 14"	2	Cedar
J	End trim	⅞ × 1½ × 18⅝"	4	Cedar	U	Tray bottom	⅝ × 15¾ × 20½"	1	Pine plywood
K	Lid side	⅞ × 3½ × 49¾"	2	Cedar					

Materials: Deck screws (1¼", 1⅝"), 6d finish nails, 1" wire brads, construction adhesive, 1½ × 30" or 36" piano hinge, hasp, lid support chains (2), finishing materials.

Note: Measurements reflect the actual thickness of dimensional lumber.

VACATION HOME FURNISHINGS 35

For ventilation, cut slots into the bottom panel, using a straightedge as a stop block for the foot of your circular saw.

Position the corner braces beneath the small panels, and fasten with adhesive and finish nails.

Directions: Dock Box

MAKE THE BOX BOTTOM. The box bottom is made of grooved plywood siding attached to a rectangular 2 × 2 frame. Begin by cutting the bottom (A), bottom braces (B), end braces (C) and cross brace (Q) to size. Apply construction adhesive or moisture-resistant wood glue to the ends of the bottom braces, then clamp them between the end braces so the edges are flush. Drill countersunk pilot holes through each end brace into the bottom braces, and drive 1⅝" deck screws to reinforce the joints. Center the cross brace in the frame and attach with adhesive and deck screws, then attach the bottom to the frame. Cut six ventilation slots in the bottom panel: first, clamp a straightedge near one edge of the bottom panel; then, set the cutting depth on your circular saw to about 1", and press the foot of the saw up against the straightedge; turn on the saw, and press down with the blade in a rocking motion until you've cut all the way through the bottom panel **(photo A).** The slots should be spaced evenly, 8" to 9" apart.

ATTACH THE BOX SIDES. Cut the corner braces (D), large panels (E) and small panels (F) to size. Align two corner braces under a small panel (grooved side up) flush against the edges, so there is a ¾"-wide gap at one end of the panel and a 2"-wide gap at the other end. Fasten the braces with 6d finish nails **(photo B),** and repeat for the other small panel. Attach the small panels, with the 2" space facing downward, to the end braces using 6d nails and construction adhesive. Place the large panels in position and drive nails through the panels into the bottom braces and corner braces.

MAKE THE TRIM PIECES. The trim pieces add strength to the corners and give the box a finished look. Cut the corner trim (G) and corner battens (H) to size. Set the project on its side and, with construction adhesive and nails, attach the corner battens flush with the bottom, covering the seam between panels. There should be a ½"-wide gap between the tops of the corner pieces and the top of the box. Then, attach the corner trim **(photo C).** Next, cut the long trim (I) and the

Attach the corner trim pieces flush with the edges of the corner battens to cover the plywood joints.

36 VACATION HOME FURNISHINGS

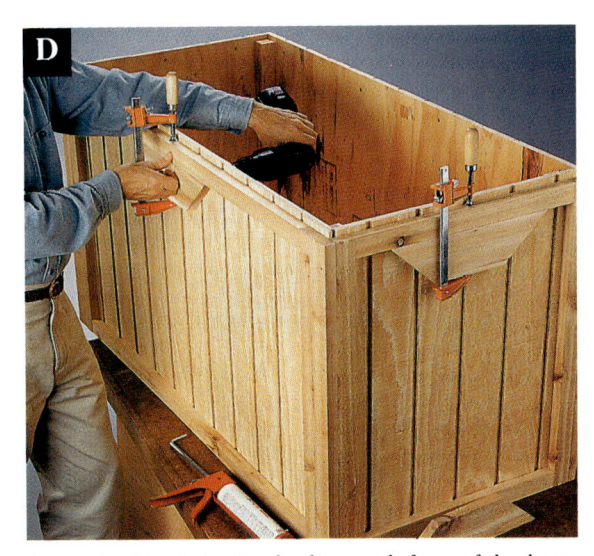

A handle block is attached to each face of the box, up against the bottom of the top trim piece.

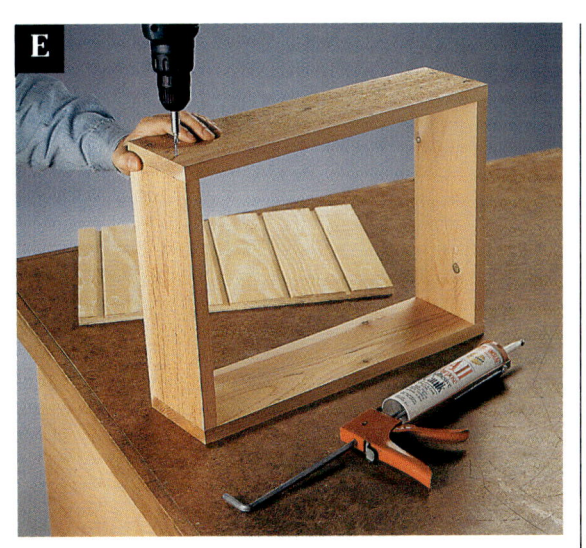

Countersink the screw heads so they don't obstruct the movement of the tray on the tray slides.

end trim (J) pieces to size. Attach the lower trim flush with the bottom using construction adhesive and finish nails. Attach the upper trim pieces flush with the corner pieces using adhesive and 1¼" screws driven from inside the box, into the trim pieces.

ATTACH THE HANDLES. The handles (P) are trapezoid-shaped blocks cut from 1 × 4 cedar. First, cut four handles to the size listed in the *Cutting List*. Mark each piece 3¾" in from each end along one long edge. Connect the marks diagonally to the adjacent corners to form cutting lines, then cut with a circular saw or a power miter box. Center a handle against the bottom edge of the top trim piece on each face of the box, and attach each handle with adhesive and 1¼" deck screws **(photo D)**.

MAKE THE TRAY. The tray rests inside the dock box on slides, which allow it to move back and forth. Cut the tray slides (R) to size, and mount them inside the box, 7" below the top edge, using adhesive and 1¼" deck screws. Next, cut the tray sides (S), tray ends (T) and tray bottom (U) to size. Fasten the tray ends between the tray sides with adhesive and 1⅝" screws **(photo E)**. Attach the tray bottom with adhesive and 1" wire brads.

MAKE THE LID. The lid frame is reinforced for extra support. Cut the lid sides (K) and lid ends (L) to size. Fasten them together using adhesive and 6d nails driven through the lid sides and into the ends of each lid end. Cut the top panel (O), top supports (M) and ledgers (N) to size. The top supports and ledgers create a ridge that supports the top panel. Attach two top supports to the inside edges of the frame, ⅝" down from the top edge, using adhesive and 1¼" screws **(photo F)**. Attach the ledgers to the long sides of the lid—one at each corner—with adhesive and 1¼" screws. Place the remaining top support into the gap in the middle, and fasten it with nails driven into the ends of the support. Finally, fit the top panel into the lid and fasten it with 6d nails and adhesive. Sand all exposed edges of the dock box to remove splinters and rough spots. Attach the lid to the box with hinges—we used a 1½"-wide × 30"-long piano hinge, cut into two 15" lengths and installed near the ends of the box. Attach a pair of chains between the bottom of the lid and the front of the box to hold the lid upright when open. If you want to lock your dock box, attach a hasp to the handle and lid at the front of the box.

APPLY FINISHING TOUCHES. Apply exterior stain or water sealer to protect the wood. Caulk the gap around the top panel and lid frame with exterior caulk.

Top supports in the lid frame support the top panel.

VACATION HOME FURNISHINGS 37

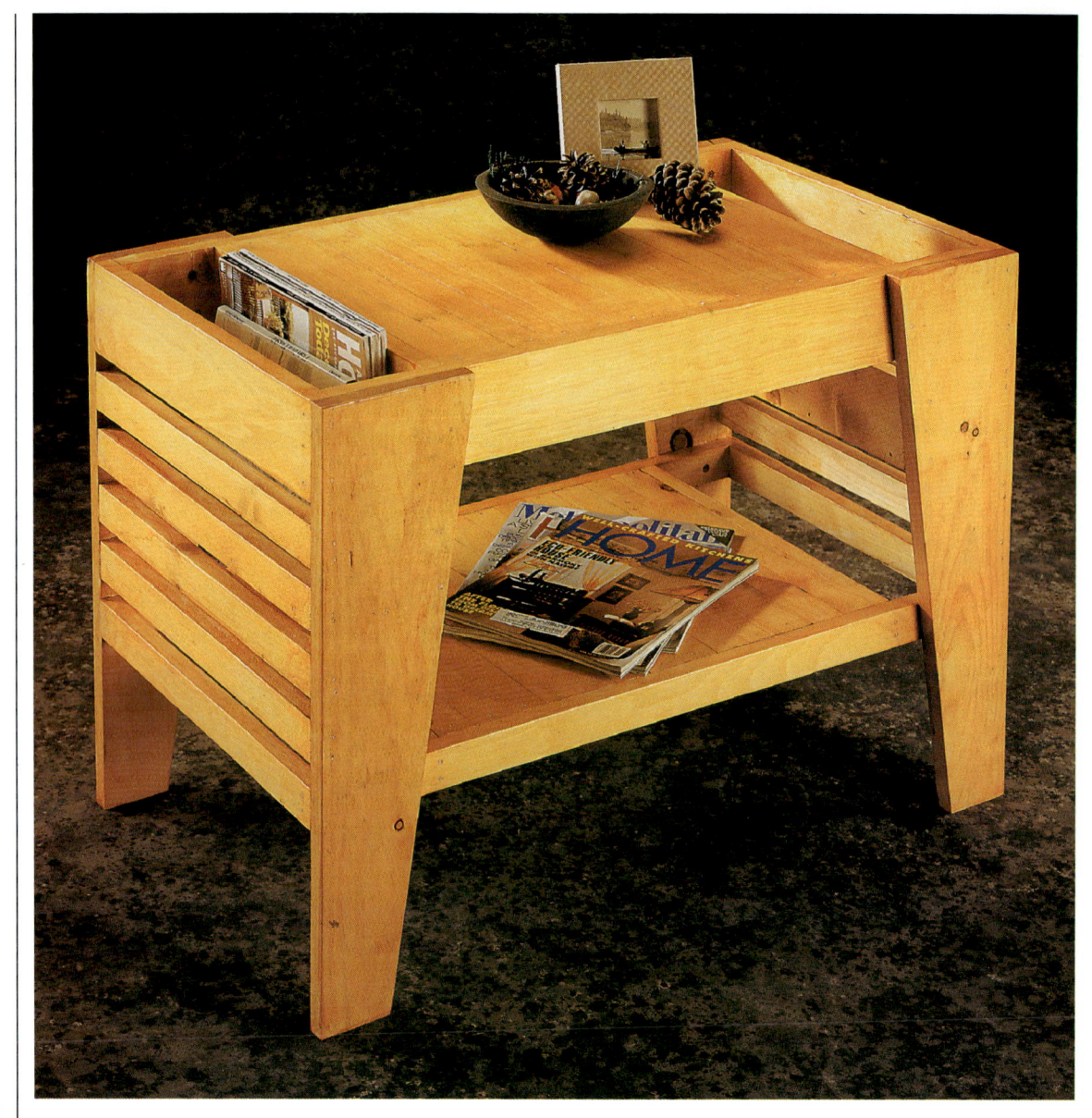

PROJECT
POWER TOOLS

End Table

With handy storage pockets for reading materials at each end, this end table makes a perfect companion to your favorite cabin chair.

Construction Materials	
Quantity	**Lumber**
8	1 × 2" × 8' pine
2	1 × 4" × 8' pine
1	1 × 8" × 8' pine
1	¾ × ¾" × 4' pine stop molding

This end table has several benefits that make it ideally suited for a vacation home. It is very functional, with a generous tabletop surface, a spacious shelf and two end pockets for storing magazines or newspapers. It is relatively simple to build, consisting basically of a pair of slat-covered frames, four simple legs and two boxes at the ends. Stylistically, it is highly adaptable, with a slightly contemporary appearance that is tempered by traditional construction methods and a classic shellac finish. And, because it is made entirely from pine, it is very inexpensive to build.

38 VACATION HOME FURNISHINGS

OVERALL SIZE:
22" HIGH
18½" DEEP
30½" LONG

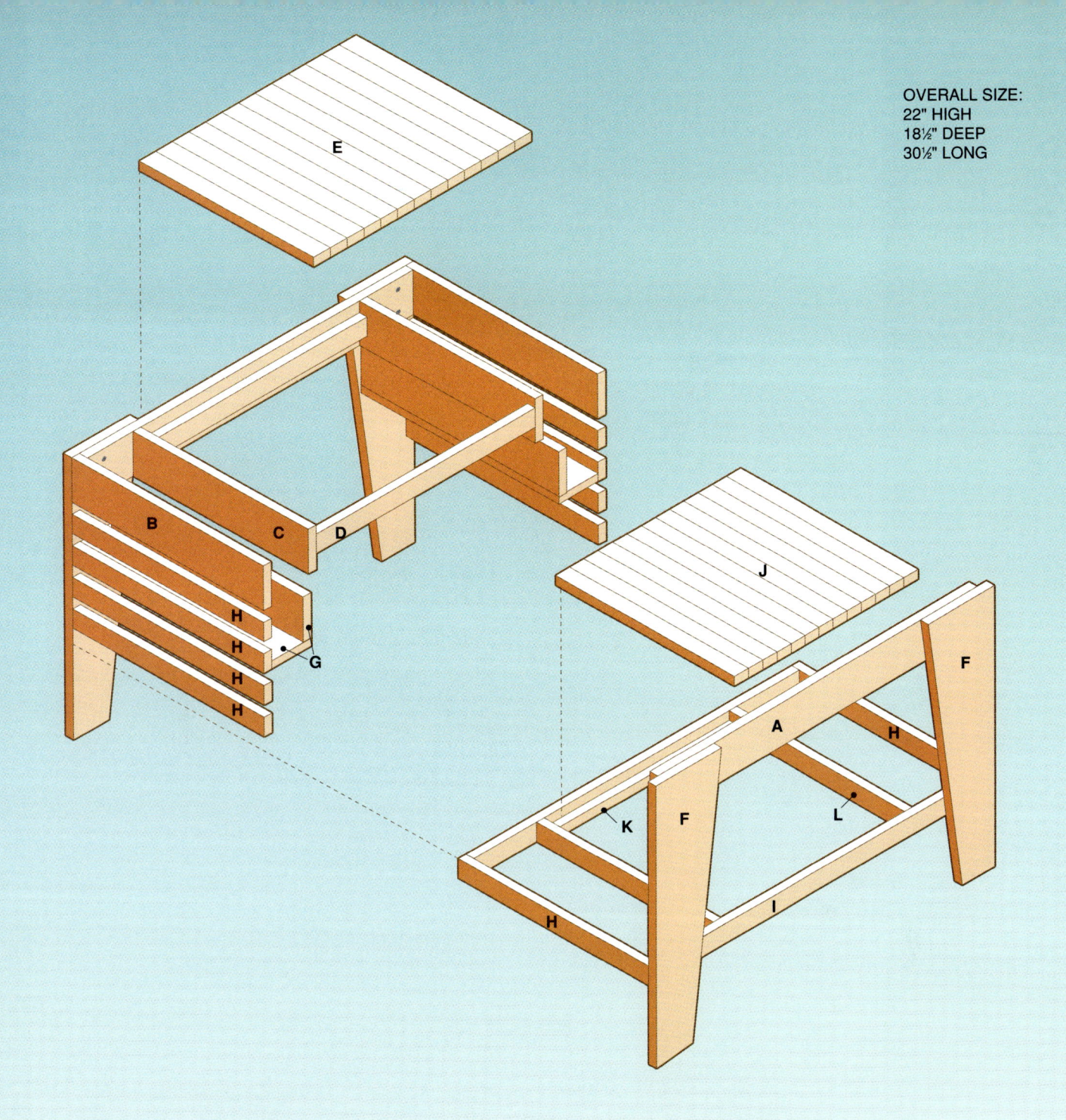

Cutting List					**Cutting List**			
Key	Part	Dimension	Pcs.	Material	Key	Part	Dimension	Pcs.	Material
A	Top rail	¾ × 3½ × 29"	2	Pine	G	Pocket rail	¾ × 3½ × 17"	4	Pine
B	Top end	¾ × 3½ × 17"	2	Pine	H	Leg slat	¾ × 1½ × 17"	10	Pine
C	Pocket divider	¾ × 3½ × 15½"	2	Pine	I	Shelf side	¾ × 1½ × 29"	2	Pine
D	Top ledger	¾ × 1½ × 19½"	2	Pine	J	Shelf slat	¾ × 1½ × 15½"	13	Pine
E	Top slat	¾ × 1½ × 15½"	13	Pine	K	Shelf ledger	¾ × ¾ × 19½"	2	Stop molding
F	Leg	¾ × 6 × 22"	4	Pine	L	Shelf cap	¾ × 1½ × 15½"	4	Pine

Materials: Glue, #6 × 1¼" wood screws, 6d finish nails, finishing materials.
Note: Measurements reflect the actual thickness of dimensional lumber.

VACATION HOME FURNISHINGS 39

Directions: End Table

MAKE THE LEGS. The end table legs are tapered on the inside edges to provide greater access to the bottom shelf. Begin by cutting the legs (F) to length from 1 × 8 pine. The legs should be 6" wide at the top and 3" wide at the bottom after cutting. On one end of each leg, mark a point 3" in from one long edge. At the opposite end of each leg, mark a point 6" in from the same long edge. Using a straightedge, draw tapered cutting lines connecting the two points **(photo A)**. Use a circular saw with a straightedge cutting guide to cut along the lines, creating the tapers.

MAKE THE TABLETOP FRAME. The frame for the tabletop of the end table is made by fastening two 1 × 4 pocket dividers (C) between the 1 × 4 top rails. Ledgers are then attached to the inside faces of the top rails, between the pocket dividers, to create ledges that support the 1 × 2 top slats. Start by cutting the top rails (A) and pocket dividers (C) to length. Draw a reference line 4" in from each end of each rail to mark positions for the pocket dividers. Apply glue to the ends of the pocket dividers, then position them between the top rails, butting the ends of the dividers against the faces of the top rails, just inside the reference lines. Clamp the top rails and pocket dividers in this position, and drive 6d finish nails through the top rails and into the ends of the pocket dividers to reinforce the joints. Cut the top ledgers (D) to length. Position a ledger against the inside face of each top rail, ¾" down from the tops, to create a recess for the tabletop slats. The ends of the ledgers should butt against the insides of the pocket dividers. Attach the ledgers with glue and #6 × 1¼" wood screws, driven through countersunk pilot holes in the ledgers and into the top rails.

INSTALL THE TOP SLATS. Cut the top slats (E) to length from 1 × 2 pine. Sand the ends to remove rough or uneven spots, and also sand the edges of the slats with medium-grit sandpaper to smooth them out. Position the top slats between the top rails so they span across the frame opening, with the ends resting on the ledgers **(photo B)**. Test the spacing to make sure all 13 top slats fit in properly, with no gaps between slats. Attach the top slats to the ledgers with glue and 6d finish nails, driven through pilot holes at each end of each slat. Use a nail set to set all the nail heads. Cut the two top end (B) boards from 1 × 4 pine, and sand the ends smooth. Position the top end boards against the ends of the top rails. Make sure the edges are flush, and attach the end boards with glue and 6d finish nails, driven through the top ends and into the ends of the top rails.

ASSEMBLE THE LEGS & TOP. Position the top upside down on a flat worksurface. Position a leg at each end of the top, making sure the square-cut (untapered) edge of each leg is flush with the outside face of each top end, and the tops of the legs are flush with the top rails. Carefully clamp the legs

Draw tapered cutting lines on the face of each leg board, then cut the tapers with a circular saw and a straightedge cutting guide.

TIP

Use a straightedge cutting guide when making tapered cuts. You can buy a straightedge guide designed specifically for use with a circular saw, or you can simply use a straight piece of lumber clamped down to your workpiece. Always make a test cut on scrap lumber first, to make sure you know exactly how far from the cutting line the straightedge needs to be positioned.

B

The slats that create the tabletop surface are attached to a ledger inside the top frame.

C

With the legs clamped in place, drive wood screws through the top rails and into the legs.

in place with bar clamps, and attach them with glue and #6 × 1¼" wood screws, driven through the top rails and into the legs **(photo C)**.

BUILD THE STORAGE POCKETS. A storage pocket is located at each end of the end table to create spaces for storing magazines, newspapers and books. The storage pockets are made independently and attached between the legs as individual units. Begin by cutting the pocket rails (G) and leg slats (H) to size. The pocket rails are assembled into right-angle pairs: butt one long edge of a pocket rail against one face of another pocket rail, making sure the ends and edges are flush; attach the pocket rails to each other with glue and 6d finish nails. Use clamps to ensure a solid bond. After the glue on the legs dries, position a leg slat against one long edge of each pocket rail pair, and attach it with glue and 6d finish nails. The pocket edge containing the leg slat will face outward from the table. Assemble both pockets, then mark a reference line on each leg, 8¼" down from the wider (top) ends. Position the pockets between the legs so one pocket rail face is flush with the reference line. Attach the pockets with glue and 6d finish nails **(photo D)**. The leg slat should be flush with the outside edges of the legs. The remaining leg slats are installed after the major parts of the end table are put together.

D

Install the storage pockets between the legs at each end of the end table, using glue and finish nails.

VACATION HOME FURNISHINGS 41

Fasten the shelf caps between the shelf edges to make the shelf frame.

Fasten the shelf with glue and wood screws, driven through the shelf sides and into the inside faces of the legs.

MAKE THE SHELF FRAME. Like the tabletop, the shelf is also built from 1 × 2 slats that are attached to a simple frame. Each shelf side has a piece of stop molding attached on the inside face to support the slats. When the shelf is completed, it is installed between the leg pairs. Begin by cutting the shelf sides (I) and shelf caps (L) to size. Mark reference lines on each shelf edge, 4¾" in from each end. Set the shelf edges on a flat worksurface, and position the shelf caps between them so their outside faces are flush with the reference lines—all the parts should be on edge. Apply glue to the ends of the shelf caps, and clamp the shelf edges and shelf caps together with bar or pipe clamps. Check to make sure the corners are square. Drive 6d finish nails at each joint **(photo E)**. Cut the shelf ledgers (K) to size, and use glue and 6d finish nails to attach them to the inside faces of the shelf sides, making sure the bottom edges are flush.

ATTACH THE SHELF SLATS. Cut the shelf slats (J) to length from pine 1 × 2, sand the ends and edges, and position them on the shelf ledgers to test the fit. Remove the slats, apply glue to the top of the shelf ledger, and reposition the slats on the ledgers. Drill pilot holes near each end of each slat, then drive 6d nails through the pilot holes to secure the shelf slats.

INSTALL THE SHELF. Use glue and finish nails to fasten a leg slat to each end of the shelf, making sure the edges of the slats are flush with the outside faces of the shelf sides. Position the completed shelf between the leg pairs. The bottom edges of the shelf should be 7" up from the bottoms of the legs. The outside edges of the shelf should be flush with the untapered edges of the legs. Fasten the shelf with glue and #6 × 1¼" wood screws, driven through the shelf sides and into the inside faces of the legs **(photo F)**.

TIP

Shellac is one of the oldest wood finishing materials known to man. It gets its name from the fact that it is derived from the shell of the lac beetle, which redries to a hard layer after it is dissolved in alcohol. The most common colors for shellac are amber and orange. It is sold premixed in liquid form, but many experienced wood finishers prefer to save money and gain control by purchasing shellac in flake form, then dissolving it themselves in denatured alcohol before application.

ATTACH THE LEG SLATS. Attach the remaining leg slats between the legs, flush with the untapered edges **(photo G).** Unlike the table slats or shelf slats, the leg slats should have ¾"-wide gaps between slats. Use the slats that are already installed as reference points for setting the layout for the rest of the slats. Use glue and 6d finish nails to attach the ends slats.

APPLY FINISHING TOUCHES. Sand all the wood surfaces with a power sander, using medium-grit sandpaper, then finish-sand the entire project with fine (150- or 180-grit) sandpaper. Wipe the wood clean with a rag dipped in mineral spirits. Because pine is a soft wood, it is usually a good idea to apply a coat of sanding sealer before applying your finishing materials. Sanding sealer allows coloring and topcoating products to be absorbed into the wood more evenly. Read the manufacturer's directions before application. For a simple, traditional finish, we used amber shellac to finish the end table. A centuries-old product, shellac provides a protective topcoat, while imparting a warm glow to the wood. And as shellac ages, it tends to darken somewhat, creating an antique appearance. We brushed on three coats of shellac, sanding lightly with very fine sandpaper between coats. Fill all nail holes and screw counterbores with tinted wood putty that matches the color of the finished wood **(photo H).** This may require a little trial and error with putty of different colors. Carefully sand the putty level with the surrounding wood after it dries.

Position the leg slats between the legs, and fasten them so they are spaced evenly and the outer faces are flush with the outside edges of the legs.

After applying your finish, fill all nail holes and screw counterbores with wood putty tinted to match the color of the finished wood.

VACATION HOME FURNISHINGS 43

PROJECT
POWER TOOLS

Changing Screen

When your guests arrive and the house gets crowded, set up this changing screen to create privacy on demand.

Construction Materials	
Quantity	**Lumber**
6	1 × 4" × 8' pine
1	1 × 6" × 6' pine
6	½ × 1⅛" × 8' cap molding
6	¼ × ¼" × 8' quarter-round
1	⅛" × 4 × 8' hardboard

Vacation homes are popular gathering spots for friends and relatives. As a result, space can get pretty tight and privacy becomes a valued commodity. This changing screen helps to remedy the situation by providing what amounts to a portable wall. This three-panel changing screen can be set up in any room, adding a much-needed privacy area. With its attractive wallpapered panels, it can even be used as a room divider to create an intimate space within a larger room.

Because the ⅛"-thick hardboard panels are held in place by common trim moldings, not rabbet grooves, building this changing screen is very simple.

44 VACATION HOME FURNISHINGS

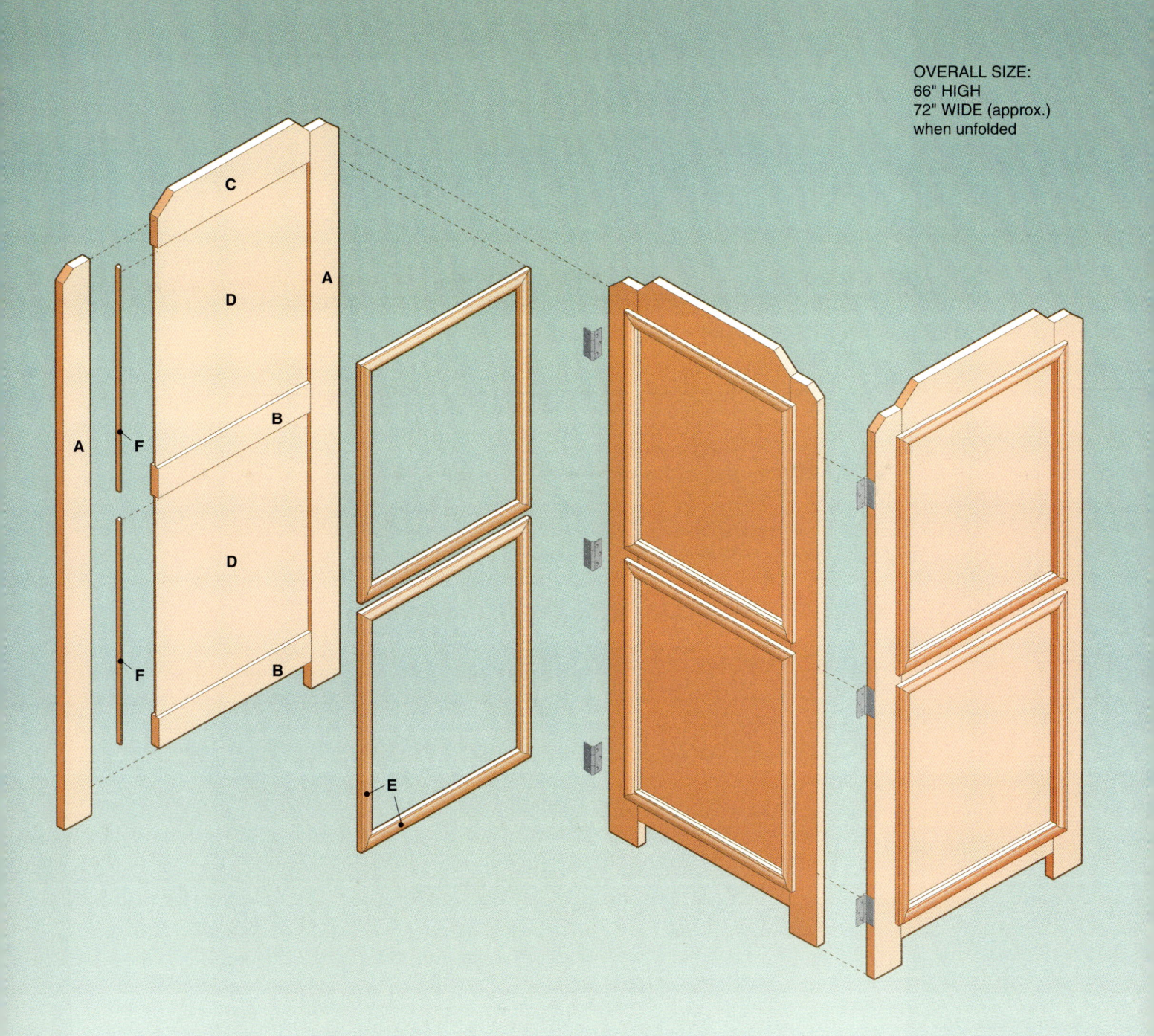

OVERALL SIZE:
66" HIGH
72" WIDE (approx.)
when unfolded

\multicolumn{5}{c}{**Cutting List (for three panels)**}
Key	Part	Dimension	Pcs.	Material
A	Upright	¾ × 3½ × 64"	6	Pine
B	Lower rail	¾ × 3½ × 20"	6	Pine
C	Top rail	¾ × 5½ × 20"	3	Pine

\multicolumn{5}{c}{**Cutting List**}
Key	Part	Dimension	Pcs.	Material
D	Panel	⅛ × 20 × 25¼"	6	Hardboard
E	Front molding	½ × 1⅛ × *	24	Cap molding
F	Rear molding	¼ × ¼ × *	24	Quarter-round

Materials: Glue, 6d finish nails, 1" wire brads, 1½ × 2" brass butt hinges (6), wallpaper (36' of 3'-wide), finishing materials.

Note: Measurements reflect the actual thickness of dimensional lumber.
  *Cut to fit

VACATION HOME FURNISHINGS 45

A

Clamp the uprights together with their ends flush, and mark the positions for the frame rails.

B

With the rails glued and clamped in place, toenail 6d finish nails through the rails and into the uprights.

Directions: Changing Screen

MAKE THE UPRIGHTS. Each of the three screen panels on the changing screen project is composed of a pine frame with two hardboard panel inserts. The panels are hinged together to create a structure that is self-standing when unfolded. Start by cutting the frame uprights (A) to length from 1 × 4 pine. To help ensure that the frames are uniform, clamp all six uprights together on edge, making sure their ends are flush and square. Designate one end as the bottom, and use a square to mark reference lines across the edges of the uprights, 3" and 31¾" up from the bottom ends, and 3½" down from the top ends **(photo A).** These reference lines mark the position of the bottom edges of the rails. A triangle with 1" legs is trimmed from the top, outside corner of each upright. To draw cutting lines for this triangle, mark a point on the long edge opposite the reference line, 1" down from the top corner. Mark another point on each top edge, 1" in from the same corner. Using a straightedge, draw a cutting line connecting the two points. Cut along the line with a jig saw or a circular saw. Sand the uprights to smooth out any sharp edges.

MAKE THE RAILS. Cut the lower rails (B) from 1 × 4 and the top rails (C) from 1 × 6. The two top corners of each top rail feature triangular trim cuts similar to those in the tops of the uprights. Simply mark triangular cutoffs with 2" legs at both ends of each top rail (make sure the cuts are on the same edge), and cut with a jig saw or circular saw.

MAKE THE SCREEN FRAMES. The screen panels are built in much the same way as picture frames: simply position the rails between the uprights (using the reference lines drawn on the edges of the uprights), and glue and clamp the frame so the corners are square. Assemble the three screen panel frames one at a time. First, set a pair of uprights on a level worksurface, so the trimmed corners are facing outward. Position two lower rails and an upper rail against the reference lines on the uprights so the bottom edges of the rails are flush with the lines. (The top rail will extend past the tops of the uprights at the points where the trim cuts start.) Apply glue to the ends of the rails, and pin the rails between the uprights, using pipe clamps to hold the parts in place. With a square, check to make sure the frame is square, and adjust it if needed. After the glue sets, drill pilot holes for 6d finish nails through the rails and into the uprights, and toenail the rails to the uprights **(photo B).** Set all the nail heads with a nail set, and repeat the assembly process to build the two remaining frames.

46 VACATION HOME FURNISHINGS

ADD THE MOLDING FRAMES. Each frame opening is framed in front with cap molding to create surfaces for mounting the panels inside the frames. Cap molding is contoured molding with a built-in recess, usually used on top of base molding. Cut the front molding (E) pieces to fit around each opening, mitering the corners with a power miter saw or back saw and miter box. Attach the cap molding frame pieces around the openings with glue and 1" wire brads driven through pilot holes. Sand all joints and edges smooth. Then, cut the rear molding (F) strips from quarter-round molding so they fit inside the backs of the frame openings. Do not install the rear molding until after the panels are inserted in the opening. Now, fill all nail holes with wood putty, and finish-sand the wood surfaces. Apply your finish of choice—we used primer and enamel latex paint. Be sure to paint the unattached rear molding pieces as well.

MAKE & INSTALL THE SCREEN PANELS. We chose to cover the ⅛"-thick hardboard screen panels with wallpaper before installing them in the frames. You can paint the panels if you prefer—we recommend that you use a paint color that is different from the frame color for a more dramatic effect. If you are applying wallpaper, it's important that you paper both faces of each panel at about the same time to prevent the panels from warping. Start by cutting the panels (D) to size from ⅛"-thick hardboard. Test-fit the panels in each frame to make sure they fit snugly, and trim them if needed. Apply wallpaper or paint to each panel.

Use frames made from quarter-round molding to hold the covered panels against the backs of the molding frames at the front of each opening.

Join the finished panels together with butt hinges, making sure the barrels of the hinges at each joint face in opposite directions.

When the panels are dry, insert them into the frames, up against the back edges of the front molding frames. Install the rear molding frame pieces in frames behind the panels to secure them into the frame openings. Use glue and 6d finish nails to attach the rear molding, being careful not to drip glue on the finished surfaces of the frame panels **(photo C)**.

JOIN THE PANELS. The three panels are joined together with 1½ × 2" brass butt hinges so the changing screen will be self-standing when unfolded, and the individual panels can be folded flat against one another for storage. With the panels standing upright, install three hinges at each joint, making sure the barrels of the hinges face in opposite directions on the two joints **(photo D)**.

VACATION HOME FURNISHINGS 47

Cabin Marker

Hidden driveways and remote roads won't escape first-time visitors if they are marked with a striking, personalized cabin marker.

PROJECT POWER TOOLS

Trips to a friend's cabin or vacation home, though usually enjoyable, often start on a confusing note. "Do you have the address written down?" is a common refrain when the fourth left turn leads into a gravel road. You can put an end to the last-minute guesswork by displaying your name, address and mailbox at the head of your driveway—saving your friends (and your postal worker) some time. And on a safety note, emergency vehicles are much more apt to spot your home quickly with a well-marked address.

The simple design of the cabin marker is suitable for almost any yard. Its height ensures a certain level of prominence, but the cedar material and basic construction allow it to fit right in with its natural surroundings.

One of the greatest features of the cabin marker is likely to be the least noticed—the base section. The base is a multi-tiered pyramid of 4 × 4 cedar timbers. It provides ample weight and stability, so you will not need to go to the trouble of digging a hole or pouring concrete. Just position the marker wherever you want it, and stake it in place. Much more attractive than a simple mailbox stand, this project will provide just the touch of originality that your cabin or vacation home deserves.

Construction Materials

Quantity	Lumber
1	1 × 6" × 8' cedar
1	2 × 2" × 6' cedar
4	2 × 4" × 8' cedar
3	4 × 4" × 8' cedar

48 VACATION HOME FURNISHINGS

OVERALL SIZE:
85¾" HIGH
48½" WIDE
22" DEEP

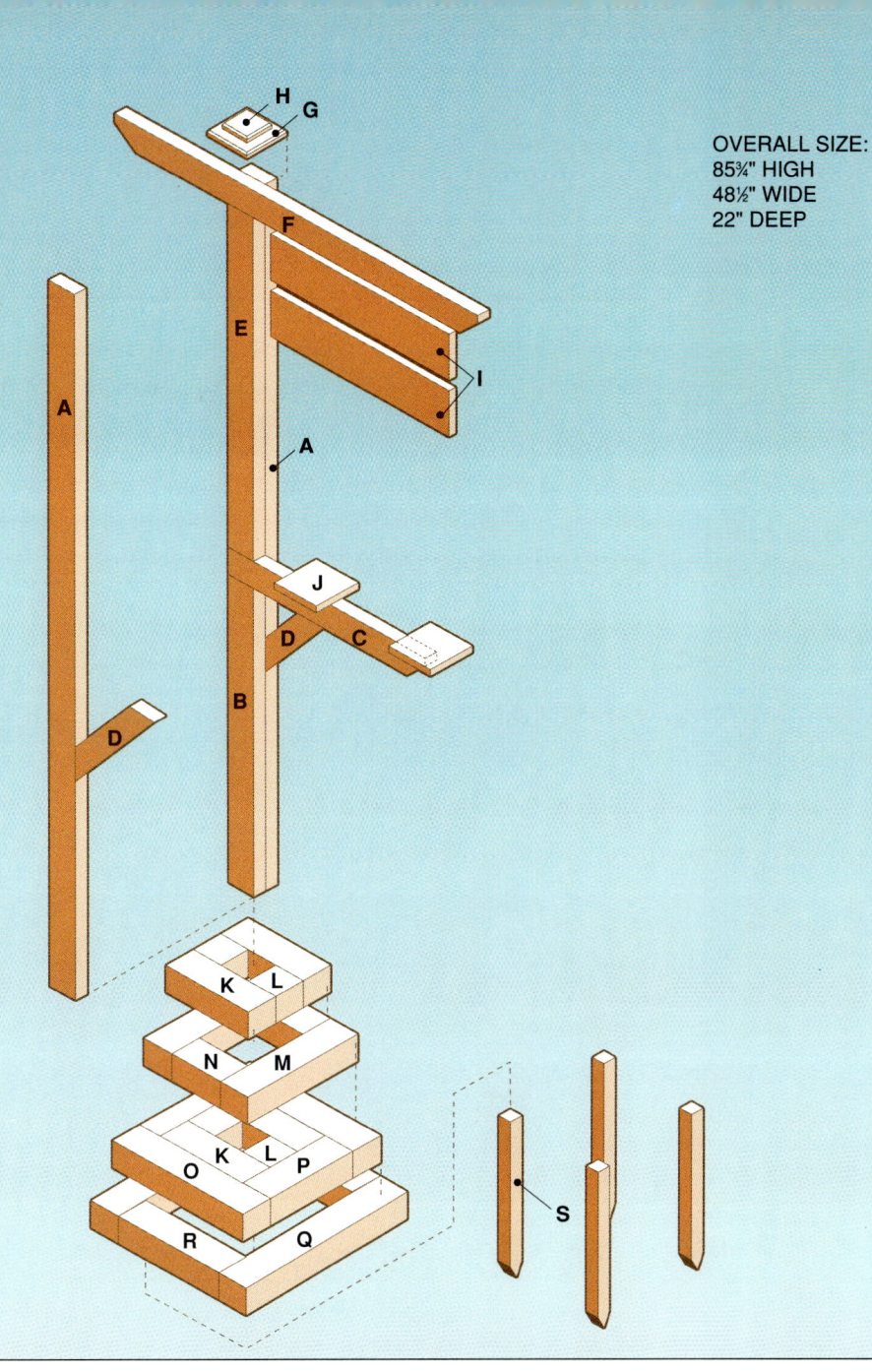

Cutting List

Key	Part	Dimension	Pcs.	Material
A	Post side	1½ × 3½ × 84"	2	Cedar
B	Post section	1½ × 3½ × 36½"	1	Cedar
C	Mailbox arm	1½ × 3½ × 23½"	1	Cedar
D	Mailbox brace	1½ × 3½ × 17½"	2	Cedar
E	Post section	1½ × 3½ × 40½"	1	Cedar
F	Sign arm	1½ × 3½ × 48½"	1	Cedar
G	Top plate	⅞ × 5½ × 5½"	1	Cedar
H	Cap	⅞ × 3½ × 3½"	1	Cedar
I	Sign board	⅞ × 5½ × 24"	2	Cedar
J	Mailbox cleat	⅞ × 5½ × 5⅞"	2	Cedar

Cutting List

Key	Part	Dimension	Pcs.	Material
K	Base piece	3½ × 3½ × 10½"	4	Cedar
L	Base piece	3½ × 3½ × 4½"	4	Cedar
M	Base piece	3½ × 3½ × 15"	2	Cedar
N	Base piece	3½ × 3½ × 7"	2	Cedar
O	Base piece	3½ × 3½ × 17½"	2	Cedar
P	Base piece	3½ × 3½ × 11½"	2	Cedar
Q	Base piece	3½ × 3½ × 22"	2	Cedar
R	Base piece	3½ × 3½ × 14"	2	Cedar
S	Stake	1½ × 1½ × 18"	4	Cedar

Materials: Moisture-resistant wood glue, epoxy glue, deck screws (1¼", 2", 2½", 4"), #10 screw eyes (8), S-hooks (4), ⅜"-dia. × 5" galvanized lag screws with 1" washers (4), finishing materials.
Note: Measurements reflect the actual thickness of dimensional lumber.

VACATION HOME FURNISHINGS 49

Directions: Cabin Marker

MAKE THE POST. The post is made in three 2 × 4 layers. Two post sections and two arms form the central layer, which is sandwiched between two full-height post sides. The arms extend out from the post to support a mailbox and an address sign on the finished project. Begin by cutting the mailbox arm (C) and sign arm (F) to length. One end of the mailbox arm and both ends of the sign arm are cut with decorative slants on their bottom edges. To cut the ends of the arms to shape, mark a point on each end, 1" down from a long edge. On the opposite long edge, mark a point 2½" in from the end. Draw a straight line connecting the points, and cut along the line. Cut the post sides (A) and post sections (B, E) to size. To assemble the post, you will sandwich the sections and the arms between the sides. Set one side on a flat worksurface, and position the lower post section (B) on top of it, face to face, with the ends flush. Attach the post section to the side with glue and 2½" deck screws. Position the mailbox arm on the side, making sure the square end is flush with the edge of the side. Check with a square to make sure the mailbox arm is square to the side, and attach the workpieces. Butt the end of the upper post section (E) against the top edge of the mailbox arm, and attach the upper post section **(photo A).** Position the sign arm at the top of the assembly so it extends 30" past the post on the side where the mailbox arm protrudes. Attach the sign arm to the post side with glue and deck screws. Finally, apply glue to the remaining side, and attach it to the post sections with glue and 4" deck screws, making sure all the ends are flush.

ATTACH THE MAILBOX CLEATS & BRACES. The mailbox cleats provide a stable nailing surface for a "rural-style" mailbox on the mailbox arm. The mailbox braces are 2 × 4 workpieces that are fastened to the post

Butt an end of the upper section against the top edge of the mailbox arm, and fasten it to the side.

Position a mailbox brace on each side of the mailbox arm, and fasten them to the post and arm.

Apply glue to the bottom face of the cap, and center it on the top of the post.

50 VACATION HOME FURNISHINGS

and mailbox arm to provide support. Cut the mailbox cleats (J) to size, and sand them to smooth out any rough spots. Center the cleats on the top of the mailbox arm. The frontmost cleat should overhang the front of the mailbox arm by 1". Center the remaining cleat 12½" in from the front of the mailbox arm. Attach the cleats with glue and 2½" deck screws. Cut the mailbox braces (D) to length. In order for the mailbox braces to be fastened to the post and mailbox arm, their ends must be cut at an angle. Use a power miter box, or a backsaw and miter box, to miter-cut each end of each mailbox brace at a 45° angle—make sure the cuts slant toward each other (see *Diagram*, page 49). Position a mailbox brace against the side of the mailbox arm so one end is flush with the top edge of the mailbox arm and the other rests squarely against the post. Drill pilot holes, and attach the mailbox braces with glue and 2½" deck screws **(photo B)**.

COMPLETE THE POST TOP. The post assembly is capped with a post top and cap made of 1" dimension lumber. Cut the top plate (G) and cap (H) to size. Using a power sander, make ¼"-wide × ¼"-deep bevels along the top edges of the top and cap. Center the top on the post, and attach it with moisture-resistant glue and 2" deck screws, then center the cap on the top, and attach it **(photo C)**.

MAKE THE BASE. The base for the cabin marker is a pyramid made from 4 × 4" cedar frames. The frames increase in size from top to bottom and are stacked to create a four-level pyramid effect. A fifth frame is fitted inside one of the frames to make a stabilizer frame for the bottom of the post. The bottom frame is fastened to stakes driven into the ground to provide a secure anchor that does not require digging holes and pouring concrete footings. Cut the 4 × 4" base pieces for all five frames (K, L, M, N, O, P, Q, R). Assemble them into five frames according to the *Diagram*, page 49. Use 4" deck screws driven into the pilot holes with 1½"-deep counterbores to join the frame pieces. After all five frames are built, join one of the small frames and the two next-smallest frames together in a pyramid, using moisture-resistant glue and 4" deck screws **(photo D)**. Invert the pyramid and insert the other small frame into the opening in the third-smallest frame. Secure with deck screws (this inside frame helps stabilize the post end). Set the base assembly on top of the large frame—do not attach them. Insert the post into the opening, and secure it with ⅜"-dia. × 5"-long lag screws, driven through the top frame and into the post. (NOTE: The large frame is anchored to the ground on site before it is attached to the pyramid.)

MAKE THE SIGN BOARDS. Cut the sign boards (I) to size, and sand them to create a smooth surface. We stenciled the address and name onto the signs, but you can use adhesive letters, freehand painting, a router with a veining bit, a woodburner—whichever technique you decide on, test it on a sanded scrap of cedar before working on the signs.

Attach the base tiers to each other, working from top to bottom.

APPLY FINISHING TOUCHES. Join the two signs together with #10 screw eyes and S-hooks. Drill pilot holes for the screw eyes in the sign arm and signs. Apply epoxy glue to the threads of the screws before inserting them. Apply your finish of choice (we used an exterior wood stain), and position the bottom frame of the base in the desired location in your yard. The area should be flat and level so the post is plumb. Check the frame with a level. Add or remove dirt around the base to achieve a level base before installing. Cut the stakes (S) to length, and sharpen one end of each stake. Set the stakes in the inside corners of the frame, then drive them into the ground until the tops are lower than the tops of the frame. Attach the stakes to the frames with deck screws. Center the cabin marker on the bottom frame, and complete the base by driving 5" lag screws through the tops of the base into the bottom frame.

PROJECT
POWER TOOLS

Cabin Porter

Shuttle heavy supplies from car to cabin or down to your dock with this smooth-riding cedar cart.

Transporting luggage and supplies doesn't need to be an awkward, back-breaking exercise. Simply roll this cabin porter to your car when you arrive, load it up and wheel your gear to your cabin door, down to the dock or wherever you're headed. The porter is spacious enough to hold coolers, laundry baskets or grocery bags, all in one easy, convenient trip. Both end gates are removable so you can transport longer items like skis, ladders or lumber for improvement projects. The cabin porter is also handy for moving heavy objects around your yard. The 10" wheels ensure a stable ride, while the porter is designed so the chances of tipping are very low. The wheels, axle and mounting hardware can generally be purchased as a set from a well-stocked hardware store. For winter use, you might try adding short skis or sled runners, allowing the cabin porter to glide over deep snow and decreasing your chance of dropping an armful of supplies over slippery ice.

Construction Materials

Quantity	Lumber
3	2 × 4" × 8' cedar
10	1 × 4" × 8' cedar

52 VACATION HOME FURNISHINGS

OVERALL SIZE:
25½" HIGH
25¾" WIDE
73¾" LONG

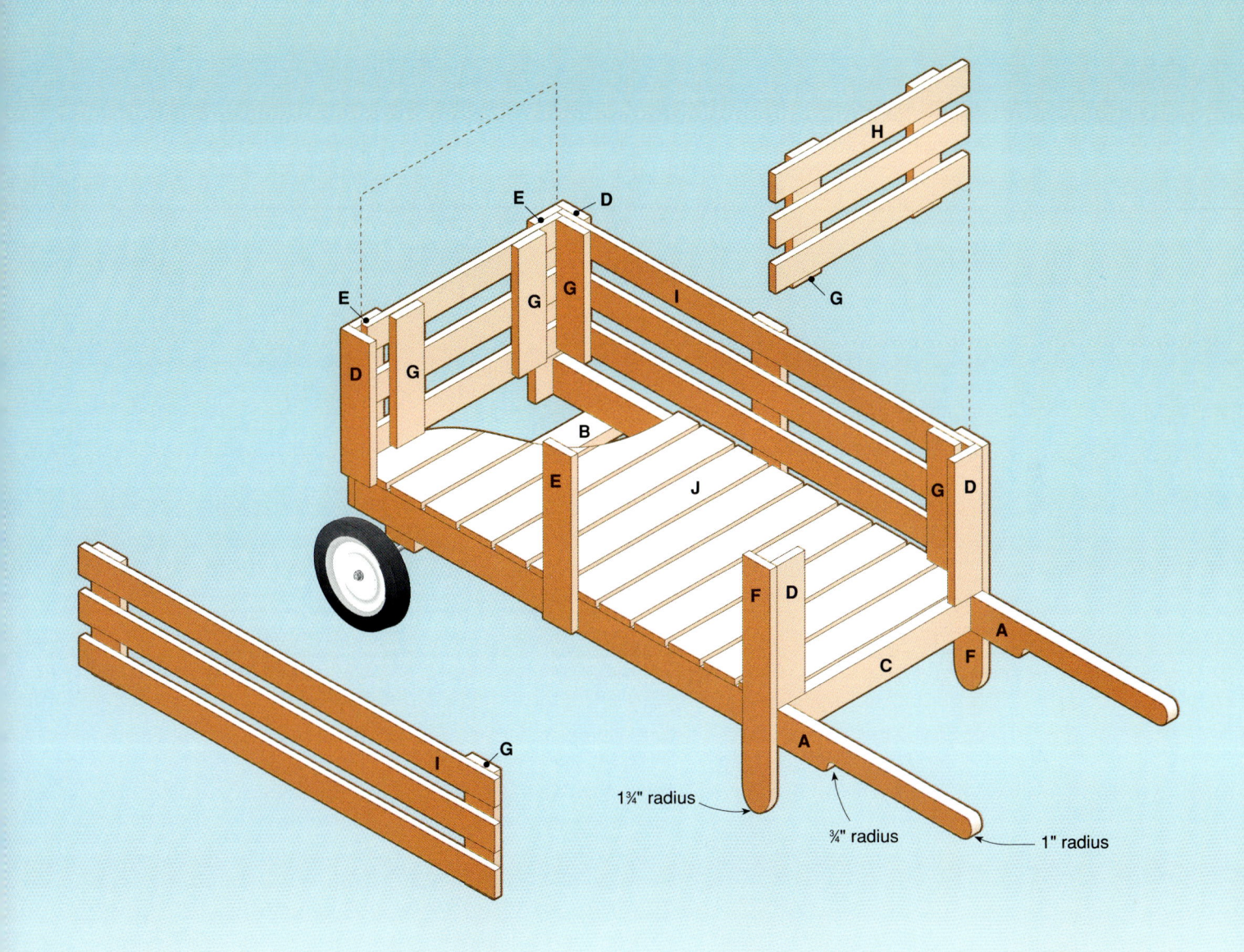

1¾" radius
¾" radius
1" radius

Key	Part	Dimension	Pcs.	Material
A	Handle	1½ × 3½ × 72⅞"	2	Cedar
B	Rear stringer	1½ × 3½ × 24"	1	Cedar
C	Front stringer	1½ × 3½ × 21"	1	Cedar
D	Short stile	⅞ × 3½ × 14½"	4	Cedar
E	Long stile	⅞ × 3½ × 18"	4	Cedar

Key	Part	Dimension	Pcs.	Material
F	Front stile	⅞ × 3½ × 25½"	2	Cedar
G	Gate stile	⅞ × 3½ × 13½"	8	Cedar
H	Gate rail	⅞ × 3½ × 22"	6	Cedar
I	Side rail	⅞ × 3½ × 48"	6	Cedar
J	Slat	⅞ × 3½ × 24"	12	Cedar

Materials: Deck screws (1⅝", 2", 2½"), wood glue, 10"-dia. wheels (2), axle, ¾ × 4" metal straps (3), ¼ × 1" lag screws, washers, finishing materials.

Note: Measurements reflect the actual thickness of dimensional lumber.

VACATION HOME FURNISHINGS 53

A

Clamp the handles together and draw reference lines at the stringer locations.

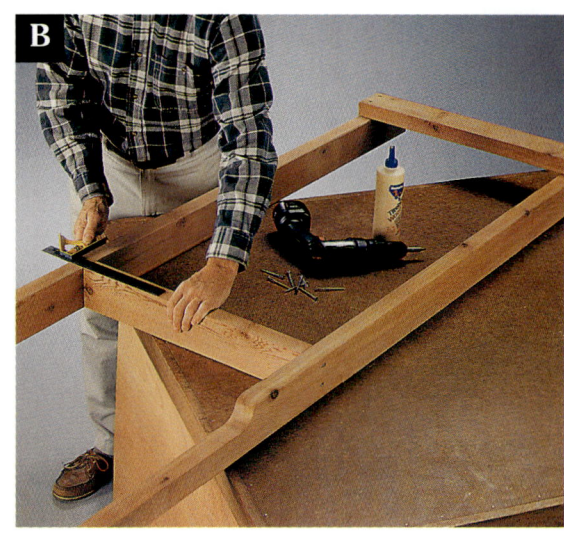

B

When installing the stringers, make sure they are square against the handles.

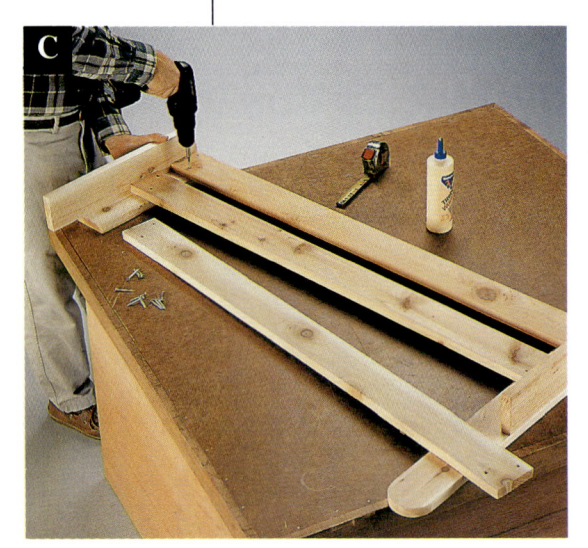

C

Apply glue and drive screws through the rails and into the corner pieces.

Directions: Cabin Porter

MAKE THE HANDLES. The framework for the cabin porter consists of full-length 2 × 4 handles connected by 2 × 4 stringers at each end. Cut the handles (A), rear stringer (B) and front stringer (C) to size, and sand to remove splinters. The handles are trimmed at the front ends to create gripping surfaces. Draw a 16"-long cutting line on the face of each handle, starting at one end, 1½" up from the bottom edge. To round over the ends of each handle, use a compass to draw a 1"-radius semicircle centered 1" below the top edge and 1" in from the end (see *Diagram*, page 53). Next, center two ¾"-radius arcs ¾" up from the bottom edge, and 15¼" and 16¾" in from the end. The arcs will connect with the line and bottom edge, forming a curve. Shape the handles by cutting with a jig saw, then round the edges with a sander.

ASSEMBLE THE FRAMEWORK. Stringers and slats fit across the handles, creating the bottom frame of the project. Clamp the handles together edge to edge so the ends are flush, and draw reference lines 23⅛" from the grip ends and 3½" in from the square ends to position the stringers **(photo A)**. Place the rear stringer across the short edges of the handles, away from the grips, so the back edge of the rear stringer is flush with the reference line, and attach with glue and 2½" deck screws. Position the front stringer in between the handles so the front edge of the stringer is flush with the reference lines near the grips, and attach with glue and deck screws **(photo B)**. Cut the slats (J) to size, sand to remove splinters, and round over the edges on one face of each slat. Flip the handle assembly over so the long edges are facing up, then lay one slat over the handles at the end opposite the grips so the corners of the slat and ends of the handles are flush. Fasten the slat with glue and countersunk 2" screws. Fasten a slat at the grip end, so its front edge is 48" from the back end of the frame, flush with the front stringer. Space the remaining slats evenly between these two, with gaps about ½" wide, and fasten with glue and screws.

MAKE THE CORNER FRAMES. Stiles are joined to make the corners, which will support the side rails and end gates. Cut the short stiles (D), long stiles (E) and front stiles (F) to size. Use a compass to draw a 1¾"-radius semicircle at the bottom of each front stile (see *Diagram*). Cut the semicircles with a jig saw, and sand to remove splinters. Butt the edge of a short stile lengthwise against the face

54 VACATION HOME FURNISHINGS

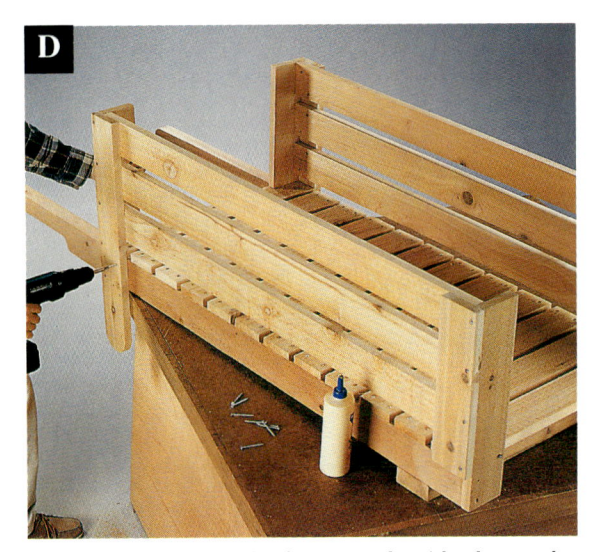

Anchor the sides to the framework with glue and screws driven through the stiles into the handles.

Attach the axles to the bottom of the rear stringer with metal straps fastened with lag screws.

of a front stile so the long edges and the square ends form a right angle. Drill pilot holes every 2" through the front stile into the edge of the short stile, and secure the stiles using glue and 2" screws. Do the same with the other front stile. Repeat this procedure to make the back corners, butting the edge of a long stile against the face of a short stile so the edges and tops are flush.

MAKE THE SIDES. Side rails fit between the corner frames and are attached to the handle framework. Cut the side rails (I) to length. Group the corner frames into pairs, with one front and one back corner in each pair. Place three side rails tight between the corners so the top of the upper rail is flush with the tops of the corners. Maintain a 1" gap between rails, and fasten the rails to the corners with 1⅝" screws and glue **(photo C)**. Fit the completed sides against the handles, and fasten with glue and 2" screws **(photo D)**. Draw reference lines for the center stiles across the rails on each side of the cart, centered between the front and back stiles. Center the remaining two stiles (E) on the lines, and fasten using glue and screws.

MAKE THE GATES. The gate panels at the front and back slide in and out of the ends of the cabin porter to accommodate longer objects. Begin by cutting the gate stiles (G) and gate rails (H) to size. Round over all edges with a sander. Lay the gate rails facedown together in groups of three so their ends are flush. Draw reference lines across the rails 2" in from each end to mark positions for the gate stiles. Separate the rails and arrange a pair of gate stiles on one rail so the tops are flush and the outer edges of the stiles are on the reference lines, then fasten using glue and 1⅝" screws driven through the stiles into the rail. Place two more rails below the first one, maintaining a 1" gap between rails, and fasten with glue and deck screws. Repeat for the other gate. Insert the gates and mount the remaining gate stiles (G) on the inner sides of the cabin porter, flush against the top and close to the edge of the gate, to form lips that keep the gates in place. Use glue and 1½" screws driven through the gate stiles and into the rails. Slide the gates into the cabin porter, and check to be sure they operate smoothly. Sand any remaining rough areas, and apply your finish of choice to the cabin porter. We used exterior wood stain and a sealer.

ATTACHING THE WHEELS. To mount the wheels, first cut the metal axle to length (24" plus the width of the two wheels plus 1"). Attach the axle to the bottom of the rear stringer with lag screws and metal straps bent in the center **(photo E)**. Mount the straps ¾" in from each end, and place the third in the middle of the rear stringer. Slide three washers over each end of the axle, and attach the wheels. The wheels are fastened to the axle with caps that crimp on the ends, keeping them in place. Carefully center the crimp caps on the axle ends, and secure in place with a rubber mallet. As an option, you can drill a small hole in the end of each axle and secure the wheels with cotter pins.

VACATION HOME FURNISHINGS 55

PROJECT
POWER TOOLS

Field Kitchen

On weekend getaways or daytime excursions, you'll always be ready to whip up a meal with this portable field kitchen.

Construction Materials	
Quantity	**Lumber**
2	¾" × 4 × 8' plywood
1	1 × 2" × 3' pine
3	2 × 4" × 8' pine

Anyone who was ever in the Boy Scouts or Girl Scouts will probably recognize this field kitchen right away. In most campsites, the field kitchen quickly becomes the center of activity. With special compartments for storing cook kits, mess kits, staple foods, condiments and other kitchen essentials, the field kitchen comes in handy whether you're feeding a pack of Scouts or a hungry family.

The legs and lower shelf for the field kitchen fit into pockets in the main cabinet so the field kitchen can be transported easily. The fold-down worksurface creates a clean, convenient surface for preparing or serving food.

56 VACATION HOME FURNISHINGS

OVERALL SIZE:
49¾" HIGH
36" WIDE
20" DEEP

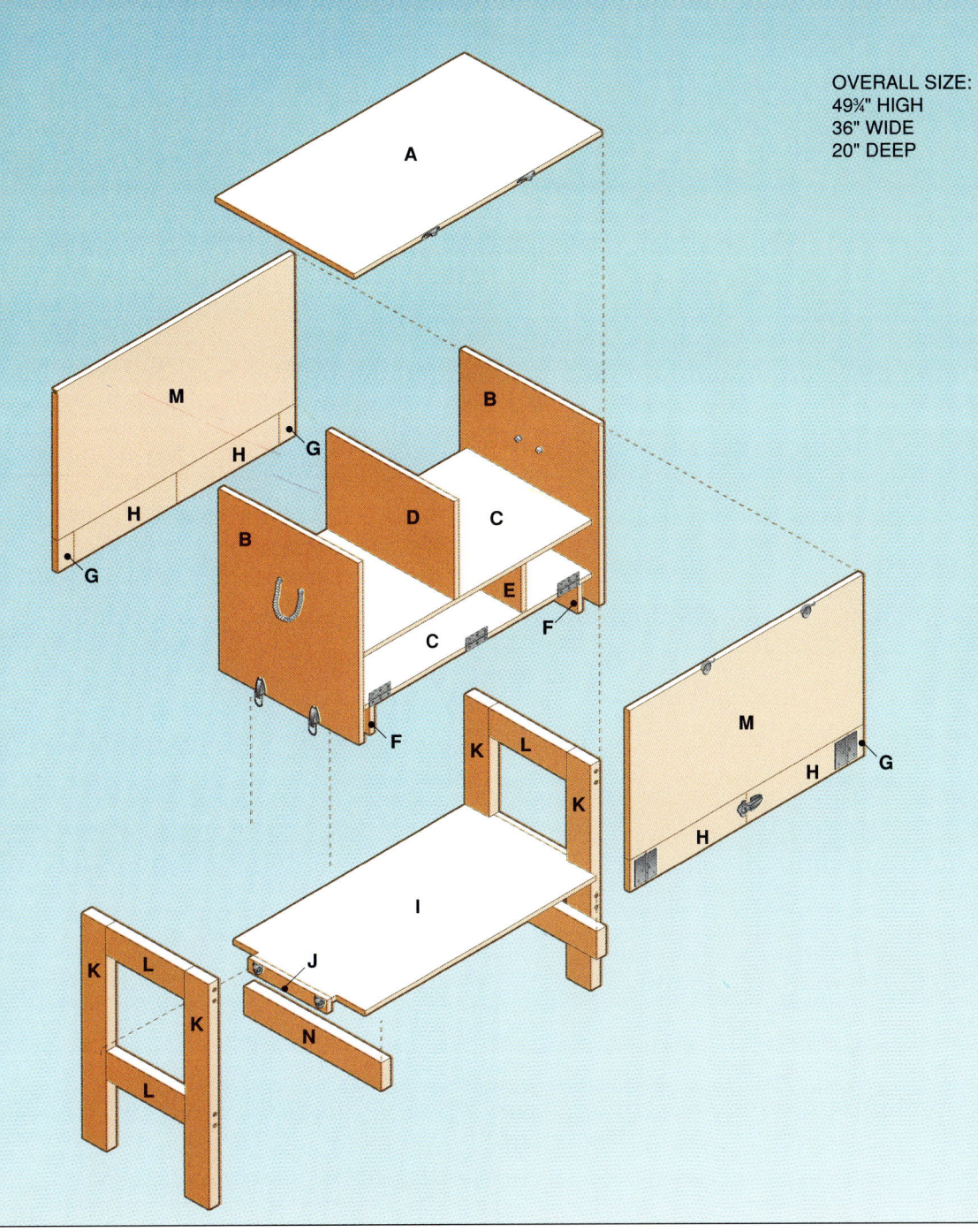

Cutting List				
Key	Part	Dimension	Pcs.	Material
A	Top	¾ × 20 × 36"	1	Plywood
B	End	¾ × 20 × 23¼"	2	Plywood
C	Shelf	¾ × 18½ × 34½"	2	Plywood
D	Upper divider	¾ × 12½ × 18½"	1	Plywood
E	Lower divider	¾ × 6 × 18½"	1	Plywood
F	Pocket rail	¾ × 3¼ × 18½"	2	Plywood
G	Pocket side	¾ × 2⅜ × 3¼"	4	Plywood

Cutting List				
Key	Part	Dimension	Pcs.	Material
H	Brace	¾ × 3¼ × 14⅝"	4	Plywood
I	Bottom	¾ × 20 × 34½"	1	Plywood
J	Nose	¾ × 1½ × 11¼"	2	Pine
K	Leg post	1½ × 3½ × 29"	4	Pine
L	Cross rail	1½ × 3½ × 11¼"	4	Pine
M	Door	¾ × 19⅛ × 34¼"	2	Plywood
N	Foot	1½ × 3½ × 20"	2	Pine

Materials: 2" deck screws, ½"-dia. × 8" hardwood dowels (16), brass utility hinges: 1½ × 3" (6), 3 × 3" (4), brass snap catches (10), ½"-dia. rope (3'), window sash locks (4), finishing materials.

Note: Measurements reflect the actual thickness of dimensional lumber.

VACATION HOME FURNISHINGS 57

A

Attach the box ends to the shelf assembly, using a spacer to make sure they extend ¾" beyond the edges on both sides.

B

Drill pilot holes, and permanently attach the box top to the top edges of the box ends and the top of the upper divider.

Directions: Field Kitchen

MAKE THE SHELF ASSEMBLY. The shelf assembly fits between the box sides, making up the central structure of the field kitchen. It is made by attaching a pair of vertical dividers to a pair of shelves, and fastening two small strips, called pocket rails, on the bottom of the assembly. The dividers separate the shelves into compartments. The pocket rails help form a section that will hold the leg assemblies when the field kitchen is folded up for transport or storage. Start by cutting the shelves (C), upper divider (D), lower divider (E) and pocket rails (F) to size from ¾"-thick exterior-grade plywood. Sand all parts after cutting to smooth out any rough edges. On one shelf (this will become the top shelf), draw a reference line across the width of one face, 14¼" in from one end. On the opposite face of the shelf, draw a reference line across the width, 9¾" in from the opposite end. These reference lines mark the positions of the lower divider and upper divider on the top shelf. Position the upper divider on the 14¼" reference line, making sure the edges are flush with both long edges. Drill countersunk pilot holes, and attach the upper divider with glue and 2" deck screws, driven through the shelf and into the bottom edge of the upper divider. Position the lower divider on the 9¾" reference line, and attach it with glue and 2" deck screws. On the remaining shelf (which will become the lower shelf), draw reference lines across the width, 1 9/16" in from each end. These reference lines mark the positions of the pocket rails, which are attached to the bottom face of the bottom shelf. Apply glue to one long edge of the pocket rails, and attach them so their outside faces are flush with the 1 9/16" reference lines. Make sure that the edges of the pocket rails are flush with the long edges of the shelf. With the shelves and dividers on edge, butt the lower divider against the top face of the bottom shelf. Make sure the ends of the shelves are flush. Apply glue, and drive 2" deck screws up through the bottom shelf and into the bottom divider.

58 VACATION HOME FURNISHINGS

Attach the pocket sides with glue and deck screws, creating the pockets into which the legs are inserted.

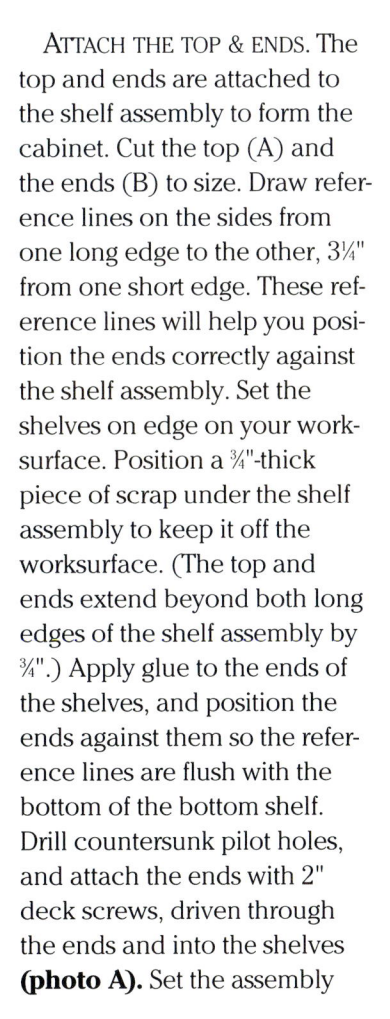

With the cross rails clamped between the leg posts, drill ½"-dia. dowel holes through the leg posts and into the ends of the cross rails.

ATTACH THE TOP & ENDS. The top and ends are attached to the shelf assembly to form the cabinet. Cut the top (A) and the ends (B) to size. Draw reference lines on the sides from one long edge to the other, 3¼" from one short edge. These reference lines will help you position the ends correctly against the shelf assembly. Set the shelves on edge on your worksurface. Position a ¾"-thick piece of scrap under the shelf assembly to keep it off the worksurface. (The top and ends extend beyond both long edges of the shelf assembly by ¾".) Apply glue to the ends of the shelves, and position the ends against them so the reference lines are flush with the bottom of the bottom shelf. Drill countersunk pilot holes, and attach the ends with 2" deck screws, driven through the ends and into the shelves **(photo A).** Set the assembly right-side-up so it rests on the bottom edges of the ends and pocket rails. Position the top on the assembly so its side edges are flush with the ends. Draw a reference line to mark the position of the upper divider, and remove the top. Drill pilot holes through the top **(photo B),** then attach it with glue and 2" deck screws, driven through the top and into the ends and upper divider.

MAKE THE POCKETS. The pockets hold the legs in place when the field kitchen is set up. Begin by cutting the pocket sides (G) to size. The pocket sides fit across both ends of the pocket rails and butt against the cabinet ends. Apply glue to the ends of the pocket rails, then attach them with countersunk deck screws **(photo C).** Make sure you keep the pocket sides flush with the front edges and bottom edges of the cabinet ends.

MAKE THE LEG SECTIONS. The leg sections are made with cross rails fastened between the leg posts. The leg sections are made to slide in and out of the pockets located below the cabinet section. The legs and cross rails are attached with glue and ½"-dia. dowels. The dowels are cut extra long so they can be trimmed and sanded flush with the leg-post edges. Begin by cutting the leg posts (K) and cross rails (L) to size. Also cut 16 pieces of ½"-dia. dowel to 8" in length. Mark centerpoints for the dowels on one edge of each leg post. Mark centerpoints ¾" and 2¾" from one end of the leg posts for the top cross rail. Mark two additional centerpoints 13¾" and 15¾" up from the bottom for the bottom cross rail. Before drilling the dowel holes, clamp a pair of cross rails between each pair of leg posts so their faces are flush. Position the top

VACATION HOME FURNISHINGS 59

Drive dowels coated with glue into the dowel holes to reinforce the joints in the legs.

The feet are attached to the bottom of the bottom shelf to create resting points for the box when the kitchen is not set up.

The bottom edge of the drop-down door is fastened to the front edge of the lower box shelf with 1½ × 3" brass utility hinges.

cross rails so their top edges are flush with the tops of the leg posts. The bottom edges of the bottom cross rails should be 13" up from the bottoms of the legs. Mark the positions of the cross rails on the leg post edges, and clamp the cross rails in place between the leg posts, using bar clamps or pipe clamps. Use a drill with a ½"-dia. spade bit to drill the dowel holes through the centerpoints, making sure to extend the holes through the legs and into the cross rails as far as possible **(photo D)**. Unclamp the leg posts and cross rails. If needed, extend the dowel holes farther into the cross rails—the dowels should penetrate at least 2" into each cross rail. Apply glue to the ends of the cross rails, and clamp them between the legs, using the reference marks on the leg post edges. Apply glue to the dowels, and drive them through the leg posts and into the cross rails, using a hammer or mallet **(photo E)**. Use a framing square to make sure the leg posts are square to the cross rails. When the glue has dried, use a backsaw or jig saw to cut off the protruding ends of the dowels, and sand the dowels until the tips are flush with the leg post edges.

MAKE THE BOTTOM SECTION. The bottom section fits between the legs for extra storage space when the field kitchen is being used. When fully assembled, the bottom section fits over the bottom cross rails on the legs, helping to keep the project stable. When you want

60 VACATION HOME FURNISHINGS

to break the project down to move or store it, the bottom section detaches and holds the legs in place against the bottom of the cabinet with snap catches. Begin by cutting the the bottom (I), nose pieces (J) and feet (N) to size. The bottom is notched at each corner to fit between the legs. Draw cutting lines for the notches: draw a 1 9/16 × 3½" rectangle at each corner on one side, and a 1 9/16 × 4 3/8" rectangle at each corner on the opposite side (see *Diagram*, page 57). Make the cutouts with a jig saw. Fasten a nose at each end of the bottom with glue and countersunk 2" deck screws. Position the feet on the bottom so their outside faces are flush with the outside edges of the rectangular cutouts, and attach them with glue and 2" deck screws, driven through the bottom into the feet **(photo F)**.

APPLY FINISHING TOUCHES. The finishing touches to the field kitchen involve some extensive hardware installation. Start by cutting the doors (M) and braces (H) to size. Fill all screw holes with wood putty, then sand and paint all the project parts—we used latex enamel paint with a coat of primer. After the paint dries, attach the braces to the pocket sides with 3 × 3" brass utility hinges, keeping the braces tight against the pocket sides. Install three evenly spaced 1½ × 3" utility hinges on the bottom edge of each door, and attach the doors to the lower shelf **(photo G)**. Install brass snap catches where the braces meet. Position the bottom section under the cabinet, and install two snap catches on each nose and end to hold it securely when you are transporting the field kitchen **(photo H)**. Attach window sash locks at the top of each door. Finally, drill a pair of ½"-dia. holes about 8" apart in the ends of the box to hold the rope handles. Cut pieces of ½"-dia. rope to about 18" in length, and thread them through the holes. Tie square knots at each end of each rope so they don't slip through the guide holes.

ASSEMBLING & DISASSEMBLING THE FIELD KITCHEN. For transport or storage, the field kitchen folds up into a box. The legs are stowed in the space beneath the lower box shelf, and the braces are clasped shut with the snap catches. The bottom shelf assembly is attached snugly to the bottom of the box with snap catches. Make sure all clasps and catches are secured before carrying the field kitchen. Make sure any supplies or cookware items are secured inside the box so they don't bang around when the field kitchen is moved. To set up the field kitchen, remove the legs from the storage spaces and slip the nose portions of the lower shelf over the cross rails in each leg. Then, slip the legs into the pockets in the bottom of the box. Swing the braces out so they are perpendicular to the box, then fold down the doors so they rest on top of the braces.

Install snap catches to secure the bottom shelf assembly to the box bottom for storage and transport. The hinged braces and the doors also are secured with snap catches.

VACATION HOME FURNISHINGS 61

PROJECT
POWER TOOLS

Cabin Chair

*Destined to be a family favorite,
this cabin chair combines rustic charm with roomy comfort.*

Construction Materials

Quantity	Lumber
1	1 × 4" × 8' pine
3	1 × 6" × 8' pine
3	2 × 4" × 8' pine
1	2 × 6" × 10' pine

A comfortable armchair on a pleasant summer evening is one of life's great pleasures. This roomy, rustic chair is perfect for a porch, deck or even indoors at a hunting lodge or cabin.

The basic design makes this cabin chair a true classic. Four simple pine frames, the back, legs and seat, are joined together with glue and deck screws to create a rugged, good-looking furniture piece. Although the contoured seat is quite comfortable, you can throw some pillows or blankets on the project for added padding. Decorative pine-tree cutouts on the leg frames and back frame add to the down-home charm.

62 VACATION HOME FURNISHINGS

OVERALL SIZE:
36" HIGH
29½" DEEP
36½" WIDE

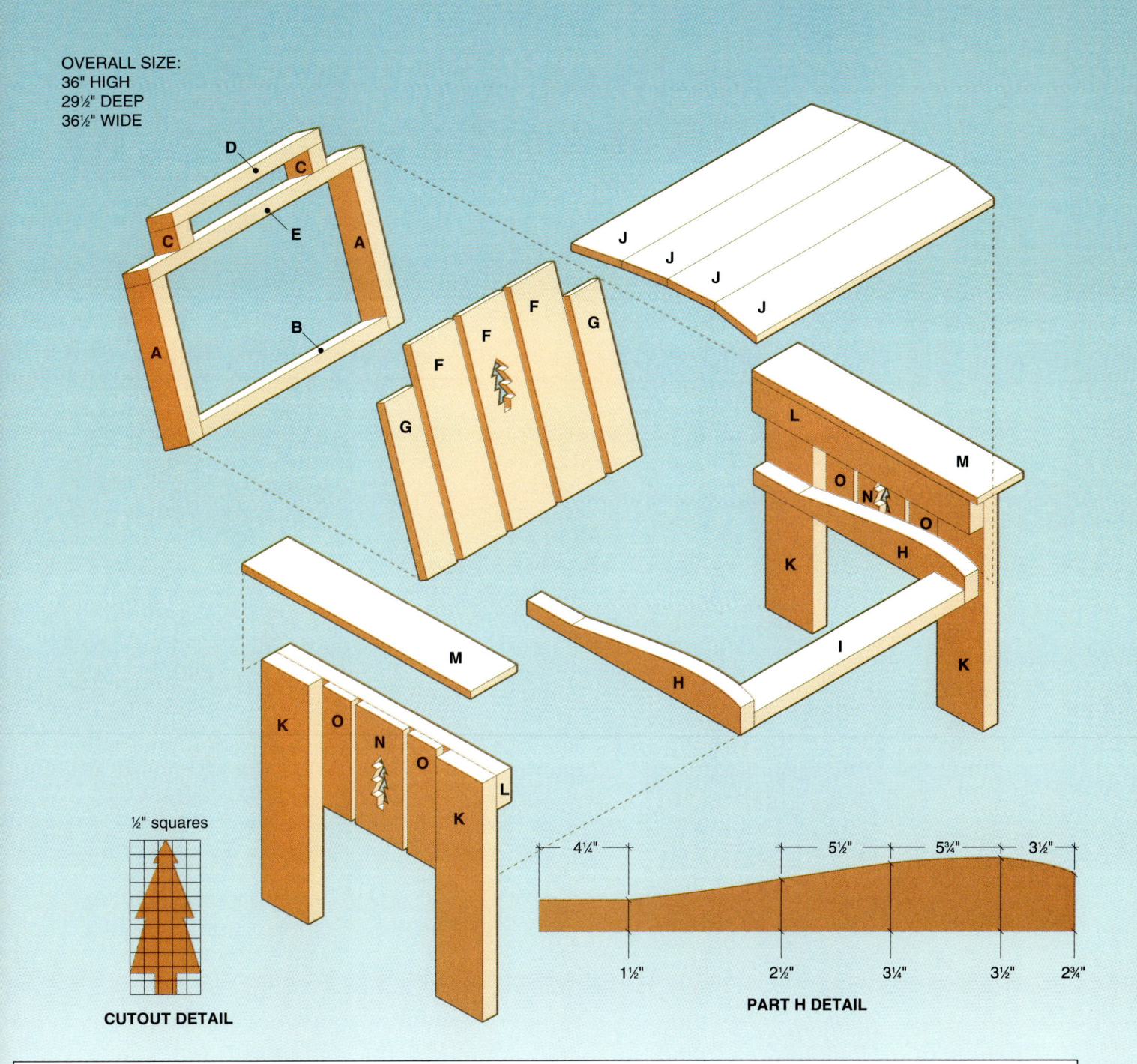

CUTOUT DETAIL — ½" squares

PART H DETAIL — 4¼", 5½", 5¾", 3½" / 1½", 2½", 3¼", 3½", 2¾"

Cutting List

Key	Part	Dimension	Pcs.	Material
A	Stile	1½ × 3½ × 17½"	2	Pine
B	Inner rail	1½ × 3½ × 22½"	1	Pine
C	Top block	1½ × 3½ × 2½"	2	Pine
D	Top rail	1½ × 3½ × 17½"	1	Pine
E	Middle rail	1½ × 3½ × 25½"	1	Pine
F	Center slat	¾ × 5½ × 23"	3	Pine
G	End slat	¾ × 3½ × 19"	2	Pine
H	Seat rail	1½ × 3½ × 25½"	2	Pine

Cutting List

Key	Part	Dimension	Pcs.	Material
I	Seat support	1½ × 3½ × 25½"	1	Pine
J	Seat slat	¾ × 5½ × 28½"	4	Pine
K	Leg	1½ × 5½ × 25"	4	Pine
L	Leg rail	1½ × 3½ × 27"	2	Pine
M	Armrest	¾ × 5½ × 28"	2	Pine
N	Middle arm slat	¾ × 5½ × 12½"	2	Pine
O	End arm slat	¾ × 3½ × 12½"	4	Pine

Materials: Moisture-resistant wood glue, deck screws (2", 2½"), finishing materials.
Note: Measurements reflect the actual thickness of dimensional lumber.

VACATION HOME FURNISHINGS 63

Directions: Cabin Chair

MAKE THE BACK FRAME. The back frame is made of a large 2 × 4 frame with a smaller 2 × 4 bump-out frame attached to the top for extra support of the backrest slats. Start by cutting the stiles (A) and inner rail (B) to size. After sanding the parts, position the inner rail between the ends of the stiles, and fasten the inner rail with moisture-resistant wood glue and 2½" deck screws driven into counterbored pilot holes—counterbore deeply enough to accept a ⅜"-dia. wood plug. Cut the top blocks (C), top rail (D) and middle rail (E) to size. Use glue and counterbored deck screws to fasten the middle rail to the free ends of the stiles. Fasten the top blocks at the ends of the top rail, using glue and 2½" deck screws driven through the top rail and into the ends of the blocks. Apply glue to the free ends of the top blocks, and position them against the middle rail so their outside edges are 4" in from the ends. Clamp the frames together **(photo A),** and join them by driving 2½" deck screws through the middle rail and into the ends of the top blocks.

MAKE THE SEAT FRAMES. Start by cutting the seat rails (H) to size. Use the *Part H Detail* on page 63 as a reference for marking cutting lines on the seat rails—the tops are curved so the seat slats will slope back for increased comfort. Cut the rails to shape with a jig saw **(photo B),** then clamp the parts together face to face and smooth out the contours with a power sander. Cut the seat support (I) and position it face down between the seat rails, so one long edge is flush with the fronts of the seat rails. Use glue and counterbored 2½" deck screws to fasten the seat support between the seat rails.

MAKE THE LEG FRAMES. Start by cutting the legs (K) and leg rails (L) to size. Set the legs facedown on your worksurface in pairs, 27" apart. Position a leg rail across the tops of each pair of legs so the tops of the legs are flush with the top of the rails and the ends of the rail are flush with the outside edges of the legs. Use glue and 2½" counterbored deck screws, driven through the leg rails and into the legs, to attach the parts. Cut the armrests (M) to size, and fasten them on top of the joints between the legs and leg rails so one long edge of each armrest is flush with the inside leg rail and the back edges are flush **(photo C).**

MAKE THE SLATS. Each of the four frames that make up the chair will support slats made from 1× stock. The center slats on the backrest frame and the leg frames feature a pine-tree-shaped cutout. Begin by cutting the center slats (F), end slats (G), seat slats (J), middle arm slats (N) and end arm slats (O) to size. Transfer the pine-tree grid pattern from the *Diagram,* page 63, onto a piece of graph paper, then cut out the

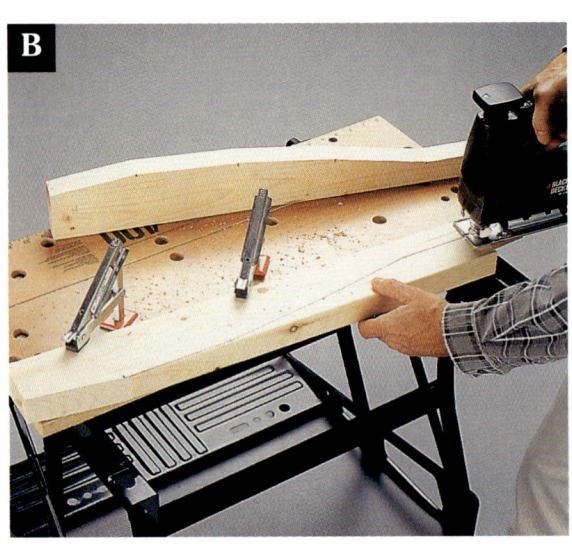

Clamp the top blocks and top rail to the middle rail before attaching the parts with glue and screws.

The seat rails are curved on top so the seat will slope for greater comfort. Cut the rails with a jig saw.

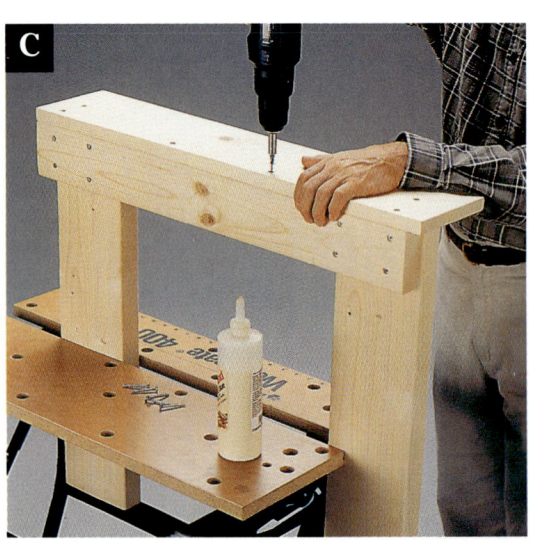

Fasten the armrests to the tops of the leg frames, keeping the back and inside edges flush.

Center the pine-tree templates on the middle arm slats and center slat, and trace the cutout pattern.

Attach the seat frame to the leg frames so the straight bottom edges of the seat rails are perpendicular to the legs.

shape in the paper to form a template. Center the template over one center slat and both middle arm slats, and trace around the cutout shape **(photo D).** Drill a ⅜"-dia. starter hole in the center of each cutout, then cut the pine-tree shapes with a jig saw or coping saw. Sand the edges smooth.

ATTACH THE SEAT & BACK SLATS. It will be easier if you attach the slats to the seat and back frames before assembling the frames—the leg frame slats can't be installed until after all the frames are joined. Use glue and counterbored 2" deck screws to fasten the first seat slat (J) to the seat rails so its front edge extends 1" beyond the front of the frame. Work your way backward, making sure the seat slats butt together edge to edge and are flush with the sides of the seat rails. Drill counterbored pilot holes, and attach the end slats (G) to the back frame with glue and 2" deck screws. The top, bottom and outside edges of the end slats should be flush with the frame. Position the center slats (F) on the back frame, making sure the center slat with the pine-tree cutout is in the middle. Space the center slats evenly, with a ½"-wide gap between slats. Attach the center slats with glue and 2" wood screws. Keep the bottoms of the center slats flush with the bottom of the frame.

ASSEMBLE THE FRAMES. Mark a reference line across the inside faces of the legs, 12½" up from the bottoms. Position the seat frame on one leg frame so the bottom edge of the seat is flush with the reference lines. The front edges of the seat frame and leg frame should be flush, while the back of the seat frame should be 1½" in from the back edge of the leg frame. Apply glue, and clamp the frames together. Attach the frames with 2½" deck screws, driven through the seat rails and into the legs **(photo E).** Repeat this procedure with the other leg frame. Test-fit the back frame between the leg frames. The bottom of the back frame should butt up against the rear seat slat, flush with the bottom edge of the seat. Make sure the ends of the armrests are flush with the rear edges of the back frame, and attach the frames with glue and 2½" deck screws **(photo F).**

ATTACH THE LEG-FRAME SLATS. Position two end arm slats (O) on each leg frame so the bottom ends are flush with the bottoms of the seat rails and the outside edges are 1" in from the legs. Attach the slats to the seat rails and leg rails with glue and 2" deck screws. Position the middle arm slats (N) between the end arm slats, and fasten them to the seat rails and leg rails.

APPLY FINISHING TOUCHES. Glue ⅜"-dia. wood plugs in all counterbores, sand all surfaces, and paint with primer and exterior-rated enamel paint.

Attach the back frame to the leg frames so it butts against the seat frame and slopes back.

VACATION HOME FURNISHINGS 65

Ski Rack

Snow skis and water skis alike are held safely and securely in this A-frame style ski rack.

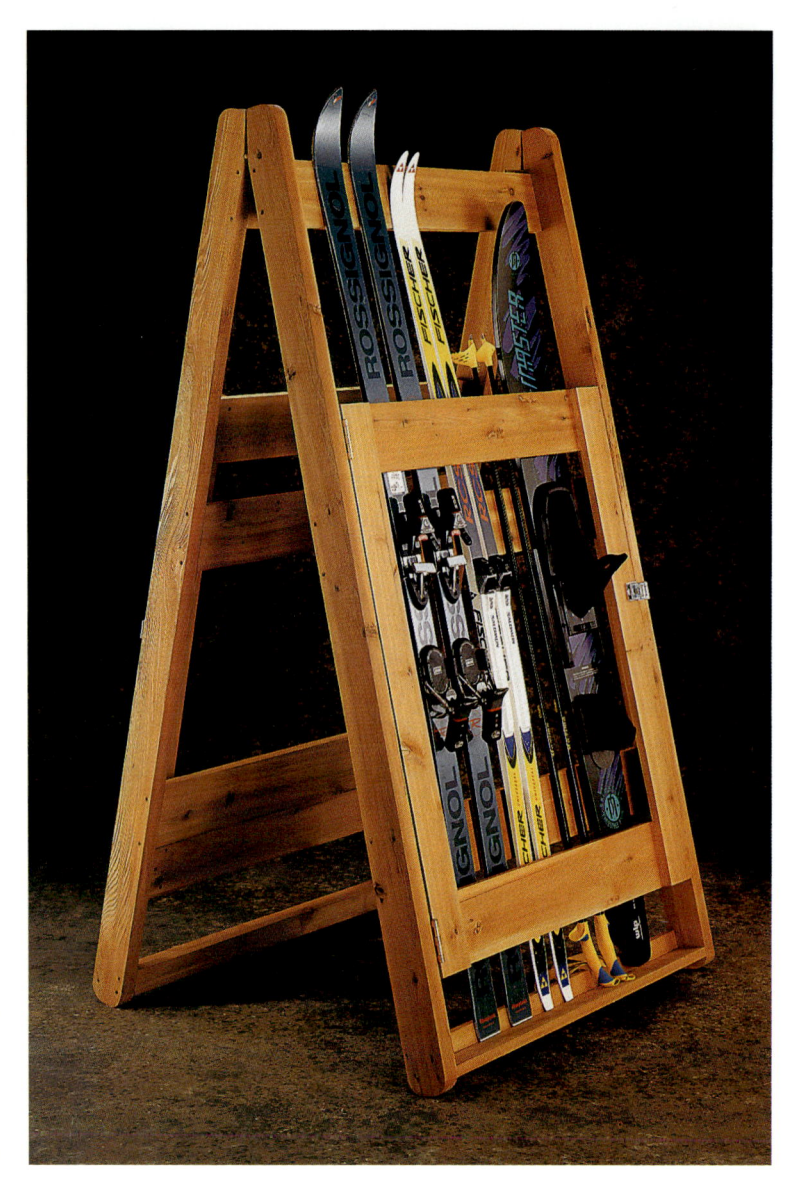

PROJECT
POWER TOOLS

Few things in life are more awkward to handle and store than skis. Whether they're downhill skis, cross-country skis, water skis, or even snow boards, they are constantly clacking together, falling over and sometimes even escaping unmanned down a nearby hill. With this simple ski rack, you will always have a dependable place to leave your skis. A family-size version of ski racks used frequently at lodges and ski resorts, this rack holds skis upright and in place. The gate arms fit snugly around your ski bindings, and when locked they provide extra security so you can safely leave your skis unattended for longer periods of time.

The ski rack folds together at the top, making it easy to move or store during the off-season (although it is designed to withstand year-round exposure). The bottoms of the standards that support the ski rack are rounded slightly for maximum stability on uneven ground or on snow and ice. The storage area of the rack is sized to accommodate ski poles as well.

Because it is made of cedar, this ski rack looks great outside a winter cabin or near a summer dock. And it also resists damage from water. Whether you are an avid skier or you take only an occasional foray down the slopes, this ski rack will allow you to spend more time focusing on fun.

Construction Materials

Quantity	Lumber
1	1 × 2" × 6' cedar
3	1 × 4" × 8' cedar
4	2 × 4" × 8' cedar
5	1 × 6" × 6' cedar

66 VACATION HOME FURNISHINGS

OVERALL SIZE:
76" HIGH
36" WIDE
39½" DEEP

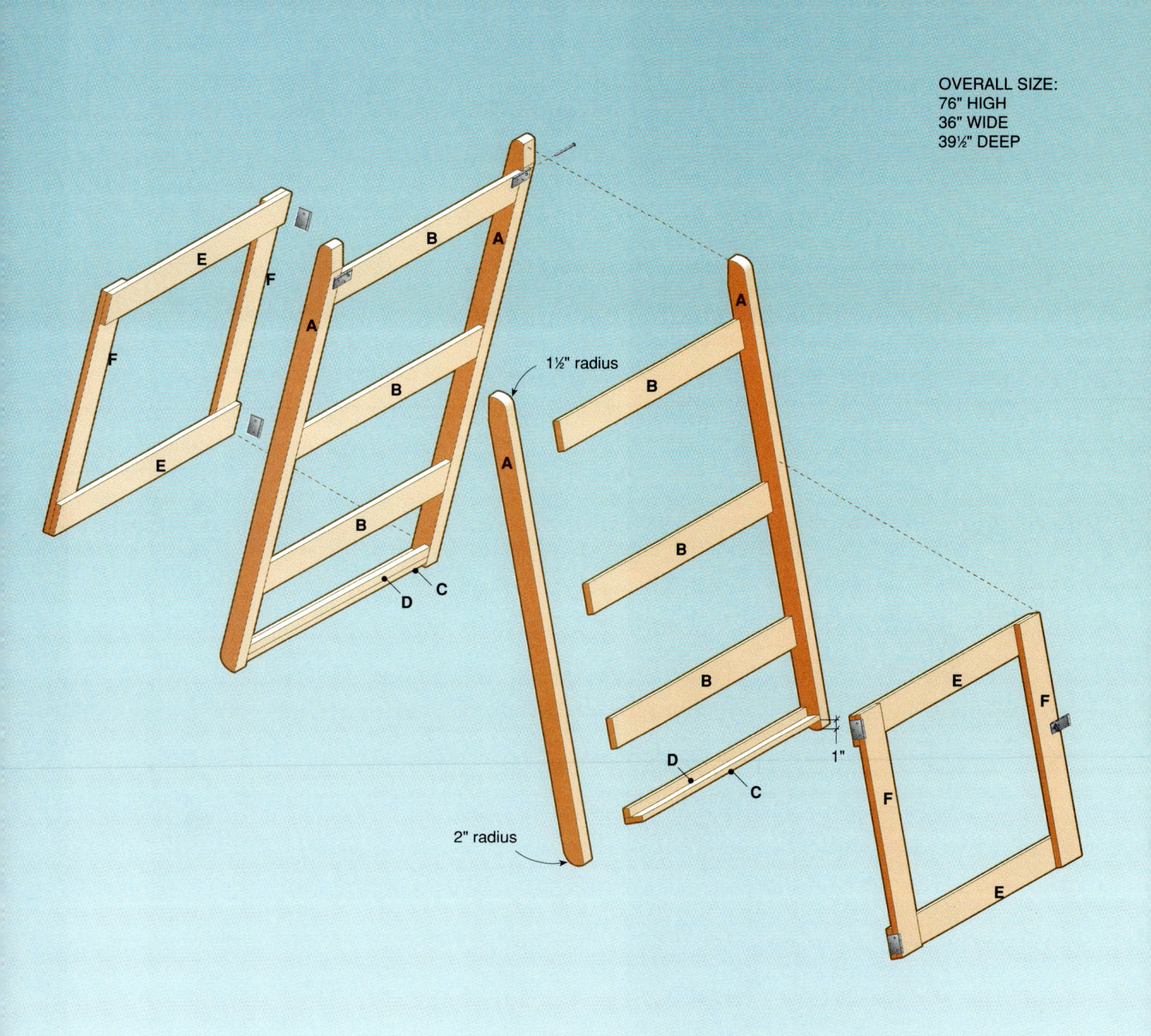

1½" radius

2" radius

1"

Cutting List				
Key	Part	Dimension	Pcs.	Material
A	Standard	1½ × 3½ × 76"	4	Cedar
B	Rail	⅞ × 5½ × 36"	6	Cedar
C	Bottom ledge	⅞ × 3½ × 36"	2	Cedar

Cutting List				
Key	Part	Dimension	Pcs.	Material
D	Bottom rail	⅞ × 1½ × 36"	2	Cedar
E	Lock arm	⅞ × 5½ × 35½"	4	Cedar
F	Lock stile	⅞ × 3½ × 43½"	4	Cedar

Materials: Deck screws (1⅝", 2½"), moisture resistant wood glue, 3 × 3" loose-pin brass hinges (2), 3 × 3" brass utility hinges (4), hasps (2), finishing materials.
Note: Measurements reflect the actual thickness of dimensional lumber.

VACATION HOME FURNISHINGS 67

Directions: Ski Rack

MAKE THE STANDARDS. The standards are the vertical "legs" that form the basic support structure for the ski rack. A straight bevel cut is made at the top, inside corner of each standard to allow the standards to fit together in A-frame fashion. A roundover on the top outside corner of each standard is made mostly for visual appeal. The bottoms are rounded over on both corners for greater stability. Cut the standards (A) to length from 2 × 4 cedar. At one end of each standard, mark a point ¾" in from one corner. Make a second mark 4" from the same corner down the long edge, and connect the points diagonally with a straightedge to create cutting lines for the bevel cuts. At the other top corner, use a compass to draw a 1½"-radius arc centered 1½" in from the top and the side, to create the roundover opposite the bevel cut. Draw 2"-radius roundovers on both bottom corners of all four standards. Because it is easier to measure out from a square end than a rounded end, lay all the standards side by side with the ends flush and gang-mark the rail locations before you shape the ends. At the bottom of each leg, draw reference lines across the faces of the legs 1", 2", 14", 38", 54" and 67" up from the bottom. Cut the roundovers at the bottom and top of each leg with a jig saw, and make the straight bevel cuts with a circular saw **(photo A)**. Sand the cuts smooth, and sand all sharp edges smooth.

ATTACH THE RAILS. The rails are the cross members that hold the ski rack standards together. To simplify installation, we predrilled all of our pilot holes in the standards, then simply positioned the rails between the standards and attached them in assembly-line fashion. Set the standards on their long edges in pairs, and drill countersunk pilot holes through the outer face of each standard, ⅜" down from the beveled edge. Drill holes 1⅛" and 1⅞" above the 1" line, then drill holes 1" and 4½" above each of the 14", 38", and 67" lines. Also drill two pilot holes along the bottom edge of each standard, centered ⅜" above the 1" line and 1" in from each side, for the bottom ledge that supports the bottoms of your skis. The ends of the rails butt against the inside faces of the standards. Cut the rails (B) to length, sand the cuts smooth, and slightly round the corners and edges with your sander. Lay the standards in pairs on a flat worksurface, about 3' apart, with the beveled edges facing up. Arrange the rails between the pairs of standards so the lower rail edges are on the 14", 38", and 67" reference lines, and the ends of the rails align with the pilot holes. Apply glue to the rail edges, and attach with 2½" deck screws driven through the pilot holes and into the rail ends **(photo B)**. Check the rack frequently to make sure it is square as you attach the rails.

ATTACH THE BOTTOM LEDGE. The bottom ledge supports the ski bottoms in the rack. It is fitted with a thin rail on the back edge that prevents skis from slipping off. Cut the bottom ledges (C) and bottom rails (D) to size, and sand each piece. Apply glue to the ends of the ledges and position them between the standards in each pair, just above each 1" reference line. Attach the ledges with 2½" deck screws driven

Make roundover cuts with a jig saw, and make straight bevel cuts with a circular saw.

Fasten the rails between the standards with moisture-resistant wood glue and deck screws.

Keep hinges hidden from view by fastening the gate to the inner face of the leg.

Tap the hinge pins into the hinge barrels to join the standards along the beveled top edges.

through the countersunk pilot holes in the standards and into the ends of the ledges. Butt one long edge of each bottom rail against the top of a bottom ledge, flush with the inside edges of the standards. Attach the rails with glue and screws driven through the pilot holes. Drive additional countersunk 1⅝" deck screws through the bottom ledges and into the bottom rails for extra strength.

MAKE THE GATES. Locking gates are mounted on the standards to hold the skis in place and to discourage theft. Assemble the gates first, then attach them to the standards with hinges. Cut the lock arms (E) and lock stiles (F) to size, and sand and round the edges. Lay the lock stiles facedown on your worksurface. Lay the lock arms across the ends, and adjust the parts so they form a rectangle. Be sure the arms are square to the stiles and are flush at the ends, and attach the arms to the stiles with countersunk 1⅝" deck screws. Repeat these steps to make the other gate. To attach the gates, fasten one end of a pair of 3 × 3" utility hinges to one end of each gate, centered on the lock-arm ends, so the barrels of the hinges are flush with the lock stiles. Position a gate along each rack assembly so the bottom edge of the upper lock arm rests on the 54" reference line, and attach the hinges to the insides of the standards **(photo C)**. Attach a sturdy hasp to the free end of each gate and the adjoining standard, centered in the middle of the lock stile.

ASSEMBLE THE SKI RACK. The ski rack is essentially two frames that hinge together at the top so they can be folded together for storage. Assembling the rack is accomplished by installing the hinges at the top so the beveled ends of the standards join together neatly. Attach one plate from a 3 × 3" loose-pin hinge along the top edge of each standard, just below the bevel cut, so the barrel of the hinge is just hanging over the top edge of the upper rail. Move the hinge along the rail so at least one screw penetrates the standard, while the remaining screws penetrate the rail, and fasten the other hinge plate. Take care to accurately position the hinges so they will mate together smoothly. Stand the racks up on their sides so the standards meet at the top, and install the hinge pins **(photo D)**.

APPLY FINISHING TOUCHES. Finish-sand all wood surfaces, then apply a penetrating exterior stain to preserve the wood (because the ski rack is made from cedar, you may leave it untreated if you don't mind the wood turning gray).

TIP

If you are concerned about theft, use a bicycle-lock style cable lock to secure the entire ski rack to a permanent and immovable object, like a tree or deck railing. Skis are expensive, and an ambitious thief might be tempted to remove the entire rack, with its contents.

Dart Board Cabinet

For providing entertainment on rainy days or after a fun-filled day on the trails, this dart board cabinet is right on target.

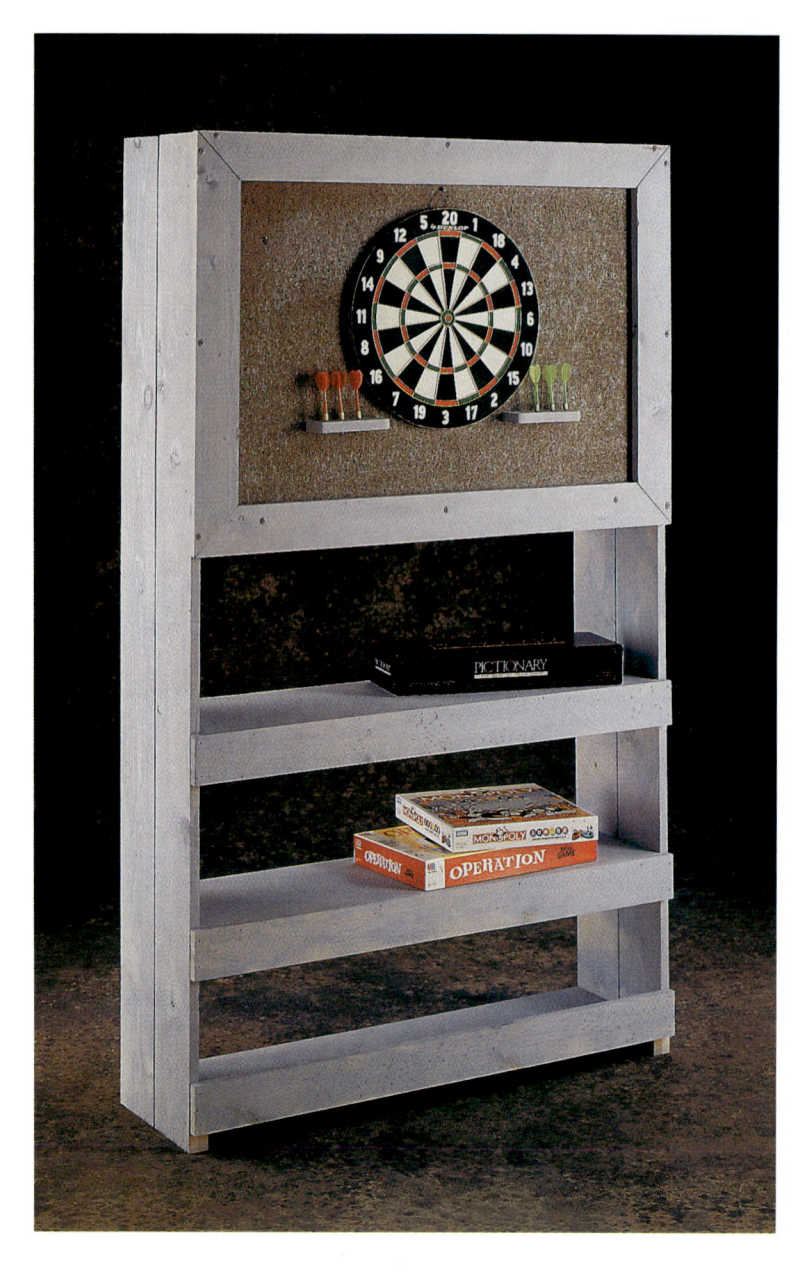

PROJECT POWER TOOLS

Creating entertainment when the weather outdoors is not cooperating is always a challenge when you're on vacation. For those times when reading a book or playing cards doesn't appeal to you or your family, here is just the item you'll need. With a framed dart board on top and shelves for storing games below, this dart board cabinet is sure to become a popular spot in your vacation home.

Less than 12" deep from front to back, this cabinet occupies only 3 square feet of floor space. And the construction of this project is remarkably simple. Cleated shelves hold the cabinet together, and a nailing strip in back allows you to anchor it to any wall.

As shown, this dart board cabinet stands 6' high. When resting on the ground, it will support a dart board at just under 5' above the floor. If you prefer to play regulation-style darts, simply add a second nailing strip and hang the cabinet from your wall so the top is about 7½' above the floor, then hang your dart board so the bull's-eye is exactly 6' up. Make a starting line on the floor 92" from the front of the board, and let the darts fly where they may.

CONSTRUCTION MATERIALS

Quantity	Lumber
3	1 × 2" × 8' pine
3	1 × 4" × 8' pine
4	1 × 6" × 6' pine
1	¾" × 4 × 8' plywood
1	¾" × 4 × 8' fiberboard

70 VACATION HOME FURNISHINGS

OVERALL SIZE:
72" HIGH
42" WIDE
11⅞" DEEP

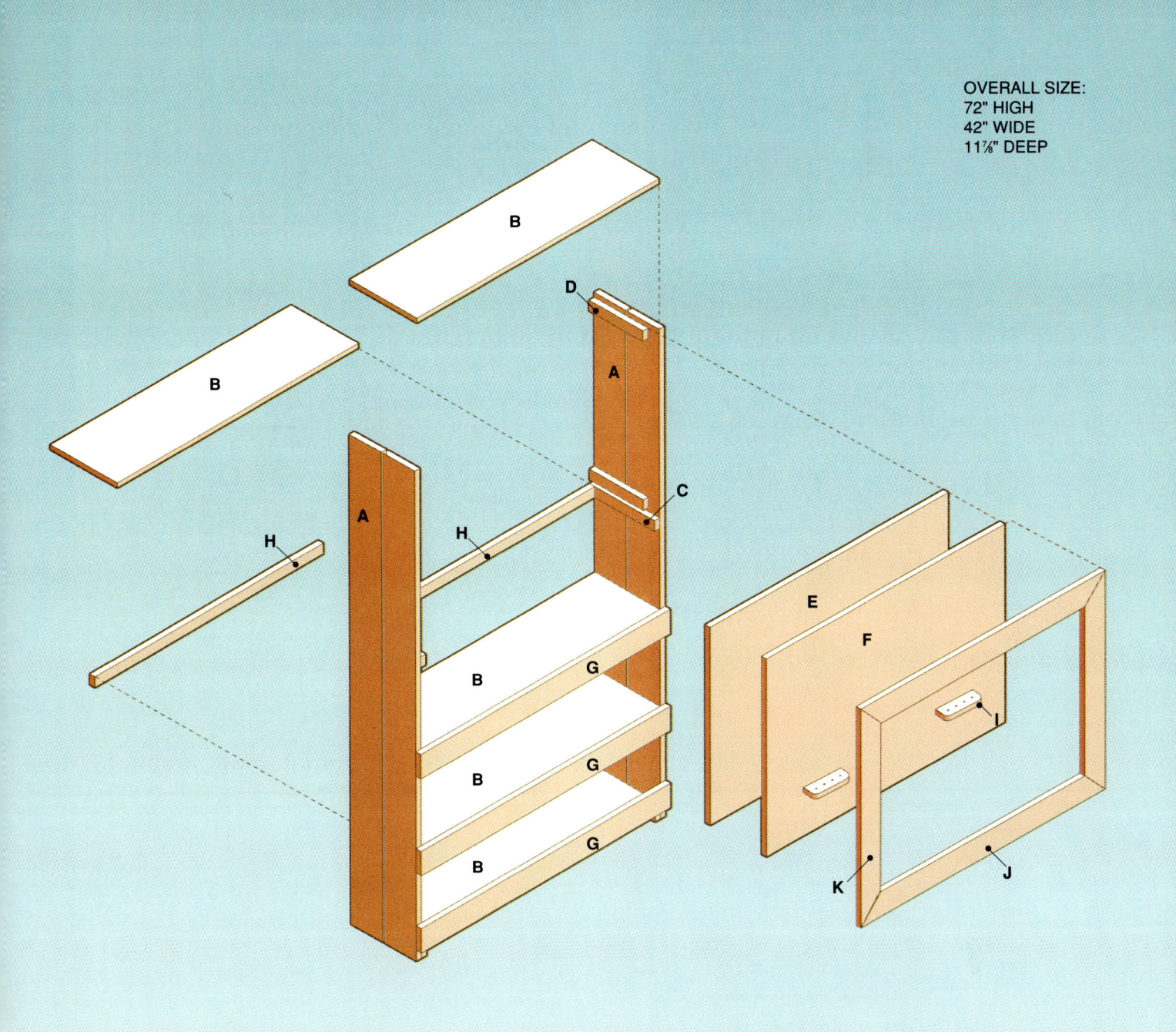

		Cutting List		
Key	**Part**	**Dimension**	**Pcs.**	**Material**
A	Side board	¾ × 5½ × 72"	4	Pine
B	Shelf	¾ × 11⅛ × 40½"	5	Plywood
C	Long cleat	¾ × 1½ × 11⅛"	8	Pine
D	Short cleat	¾ × 1½ × 9⅝"	4	Pine
E	Backer board	¾ × 26¼ × 40½"	1	Plywood
F	Face board	¼ × 26¼ × 40½"	1	Fiberboard

		Cutting List		
Key	**Part**	**Dimension**	**Pcs.**	**Material**
G	Shelf front	¾ × 3½ × 42"	3	Pine
H	Nailing strip	¾ × 1½ × 39"	2	Pine
I	Dart holder	¾ × 1½ × 6"	2	Pine
J	Long frame board	¾ × 3½ × 42"	2	Pine
K	Short frame board	¾ × 3½ × 29¼"	2	Pine

Materials: Glue, #6 × 1¼" wood screws, decorative washers (12), 6d finish nails, finishing materials.

Note: Measurements reflect the actual thickness of dimensional lumber.

VACATION HOME FURNISHINGS 71

A

Leave a ¾"-wide gap for a shelf board between the highest long cleats and the lower short cleats.

B

Install the highest and lowest shelves first to square up the cabinet, then install the intermediate shelves.

Directions: Dart Board Cabinet

MAKE THE SIDES. The cabinet sides are each made from a pair of 1 × 6 boards held together with shelf cleats. A narrow gap is left between the side boards. Start by cutting the side boards (A), long cleats (C) and short cleats (D) to length. Sand all parts after cutting. To make sure the shelf cleats are aligned, mark their locations on all four side boards at one time. Clamp the side boards together edge to edge on a flat worksurface, making sure the edges are flush. Mark reference lines at the shelf cleat heights across all four boards: 1½", 15", 28¾", 43½" and 44¼" up from one end (this will be the bottom) and 2¼" down from the opposite (top) end. Unclamp the side boards, and position them together in pairs, edge to edge and flush at the ends. Slip ⅛"-thick spacers between the side boards, and clamp them together in pairs. Attach the long cleats at the lower four cleat position lines, so the bottom edges of the cleats are flush with the lines and the ends are flush with the edges of the side board pairs. Drill countersunk pilot holes through the cleats, and attach them with #6 × 1¼" wood screws. Attach the short cleats (D) so their bottom edges are flush with the top two reference lines **(photo A)**, making sure their back edges are flush with the back edges of the side board pairs. Note that there is a ¾"-wide gap between the highest long cleats and the lower short cleats.

ATTACH THE SHELVES. The shelves are cut from plywood and attached to the cleats with glue and finish nails. Strips of shelf nosing cut from 1 × 4 pine are attached to the front edges of the shelves to conceal the plywood edges. Cut the shelves (B) to size from ¾"-thick plywood. With the side board pairs spaced 40½" apart, attach the shelves to the cleats with glue and 6d finish nails, beginning with the highest and lowest shelves before attaching the intermediate shelves **(photo B)**.

ATTACH THE NAILING STRIPS. A nailing strip is attached inside the cabinet frame, at the back, to create a surface for securing the cabinet to a wall (the game cabinet is self-standing, but attaching it to the wall will eliminate the possibility that it will tip over). Also, if you are a dart purist, you know that the bull's-eye on the dart board should be exactly 6' above ground. To accomplish this, add a second nailing strip between the second-lowest cleats so you can mount the cabinet to the wall a foot or two above the floor. Cut the nailing strip or strips (H) to size. Attach a nailing strip between the highest long cleats, making sure the top edge of the nailing strip

Cut the frame boards to fit, one at a time, using a combination square to draw the mitered cutting lines at the corners.

Attach the dart holders by driving screws through the face board and into the backer board.

butts against the bottom of the shelf. The back edge of the nailing strip should be flush with the ends of the cleats. Use glue and 6d finish nails driven through the side boards and cleats, and into the ends of the nailing strip. Also drive 4d finish nails through the back of the shelf and into the top of the nailing strip. Attach the lower nailing strip if you wish to hang the cabinet off the ground.

ATTACH THE SHELF FRONTS. Cut the shelf fronts (G) to length from 1 × 4 pine to use as shelf-edge nosing. Use glue and 6d finish nails to attach the shelf fronts to the front edges of the shelves. The top edge of each of the top two shelf fronts should be flush with the top of the shelf. The bottom edge of the lowest shelf front should be flush with the bottom of the lowest shelf.

ATTACH THE BACKER BOARD. The backer board is attached at the top of the cabinet to create a mounting surface for a dart board. Cut the backer board (E) to size. Position it in the recess created by the sides, shelves and short cleats. Nail the backer board in place with 6d finish nails, driven through the backer and into the cleats.

ATTACH THE FACE BOARD & FRAME. The face board for the dart board is a piece of fiberboard cut to the same size as the backer board. Fiberboard will not damage the tips of errant darts, and can be replaced easily if it becomes worn. It is held in place by a mitered pine retainer frame attached to the cabinet with screws and washers so it can be removed easily. Cut the face board (F) to size from ¾"-thick fiberboard, and position it on the backer board. Cut a long frame board (J) to length, mitering the ends at opposing 45° angles—use a power miter box or a hand miter box and backsaw to cut the miters. Clamp the long board at the top of the cabinet, and use it as reference for making sure the short frame boards (K) on the sides are cut to fit **(photo C).** After all four frame boards are cut to fit, attach them with #6 × 1¼" wood screws fitted with decorative washers. Drive three screws in each frame board and into the edges of the cabinet and the shelf.

APPLY FINISHING TOUCHES. Cut the dart holders (I) to size, and hand-sand their corners smooth. Drill four ⅛"-dia. holes for dart tips in each holder, and attach them to the face board, 5½" up from the bottom, using #6 × 2" wood screws **(photo D).** Set all nail heads, and cover nail and screw heads with wood putty. Sand and paint the cabinet, if desired—we used thinned latex paint for a color-washed effect. Hang a dart board in the center of the frame. Mount the cabinet to the wall if you want the board to be 6' above the floor.

VACATION HOME FURNISHINGS 73

PROJECT
POWER TOOLS

Lap Trays

These handy trays provide a stable snacking surface for picnics or light meals in the family room.

These lap trays provide a stable eating surface, whether you're out in the backyard, on a picnic or indoors watching television.

Many snack trays are unstable and shaky, but these lap trays fit securely on either the arms of your chair or on your legs. Because you don't have to hold the snack tray as you eat, the surface is as steady as a kitchen table.

The lap trays are made almost entirely out of cedar, a durable, attractive wood. We attached cedar holders on both ends of the tray. These holders cradle your cutlery and glasses so you won't drop your silverware or spill your drink when you hustle your meal from the kitchen. And for the inevitable dinnertime mishap, it is good to know the tileboard top is durable and easy to wipe clean with a damp cloth.

When you consider how simple these trays are to build and how useful they are, you will be amazed you ever did without them. To make sure you have enough of these handy lap trays when company drops by, it's a good idea to make several. We designed them to stack neatly and efficiently in even the most crowded kitchen cupboard.

Construction Materials

Quantity	Lumber
1	1 × 6" × 8' cedar
1	1 × 4" × 6' cedar
1	1 × 2" × 6' cedar
1	⅛" × 2 × 4' tileboard

74 VACATION HOME FURNISHINGS

OVERALL SIZE:
2¾" HIGH
14½" DEEP
26" LONG

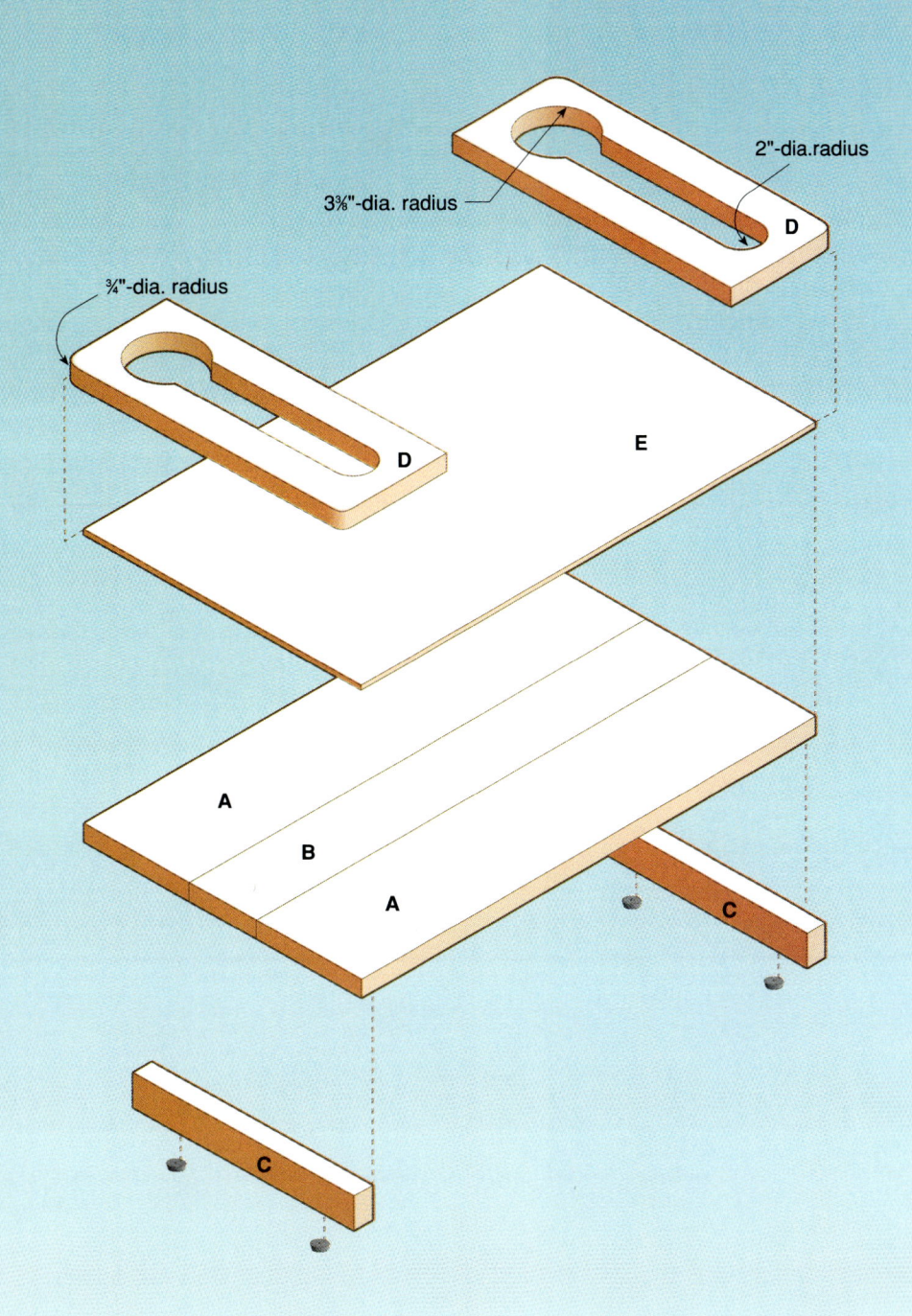

¾"-dia. radius

3⅜"-dia. radius

2"-dia. radius

Cutting List				
Key	Part	Dimension	Pcs.	Material
A	Base side	⅞ × 5½ × 24"	2	Cedar
B	Base middle	⅞ × 3½ × 24"	1	Cedar
C	Leg	⅞ × 1½ × 11½"	2	Cedar

Cutting List				
Key	Part	Dimension	Pcs.	Material
D	Holder	⅞ × 5½ × 14½"	2	Cedar
E	Top	⅞ × 14½ × 24"	1	Tileboard

Materials: 1⅝" deck screws, finish nails (3d), wood glue, construction adhesive, all-purpose caulk, ¾"-dia. rubber feet (4), finishing materials.

Note: Measurements reflect the actual thickness of dimensional lumber.

VACATION HOME FURNISHINGS

Directions: Lap Trays

MAKE THE TRAY BASE. The tray base is made of three boards laid together edge to edge. The base is then covered with tileboard to create an easy-to-clean surface. Begin by cutting the base sides (A), base middle (B) and legs (C) to size. Sand all parts after cutting to remove any rough edges. Position the base middle between the base sides so their ends are flush. Draw reference lines across the workpieces, 1⅛" in from each end, to mark the positions of the legs. Remove the clamps, and drill countersunk pilot holes through the base sides and base middle to attach the legs. Apply moisture-resistant glue to the legs, and position them onto the base sides and base middle **(photo A)**. The outside edges of the legs should be flush with the reference lines. Fasten the legs with 1⅝" deck screws. Sand any sharp edges smooth.

MAKE THE HOLDERS. The holders are 1 × 6 boards that are fastened at each end of the tray. A keyhole-shaped cutout is made on each holder for silverware and glassware. Cut the holders (D) to length. Before shaping the holders, position them together side by side, so the ends are flush. Use a compass to draw a ¾"-radius curve on the outside corners of the holders. Cut the curves with a jig saw. Draw reference lines across the holders, 2¼" in from one end and 2⅝" in from the opposite end. On each holder, draw a 1"-radius circle, centered on the 2¼" reference line; draw a 1¾"-radius circle, centered on the 2⅝" reference line. Next, use a combination square to draw straight reference lines, 1¾" in from each long edge. These reference lines should be parallel to the long edges of the holders and connect the circles drawn on the workpieces (see *Diagram*). Clamp the holders to your worksurface, and drill a ⅜"-dia. starter hole inside the

> **TIP**
>
> *Tileboard adhesives are relatively easy to use and come in cartridges to be used with a caulking gun. These materials require a lot of ventilation, so use them carefully. Apply tileboard adhesive with a caulking gun, then position the tileboard in place. After the tileboard is in position, use a wallpaper roller, or J-roller, to distribute pressure, spreading the tileboard adhesive evenly under the tileboard surface; make sure to start at the center and work your way out as you go.*

Apply glue to the legs, position them onto the base sides and base middle, then fasten them with screws.

Draw the cutout shapes on the holders, then cut them with a jig saw.

Apply a thin layer of tileboard adhesive to the base, and position the top in place.

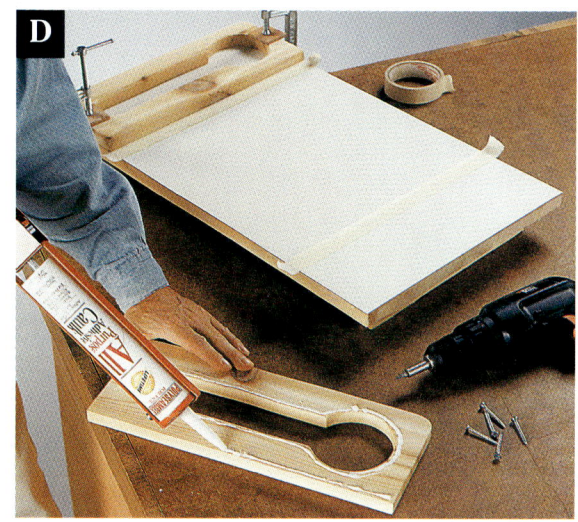

Use tape to mark positions on the tileboard for the holders, then attach them with caulk and screws.

cutout area, then cut with a jig saw **(photo B).** Sand the edges of the cutout areas with a 1½"-dia. drum sander attachment on your electric drill, or hand-sand with medium-grit sandpaper and a small sanding block.

ASSEMBLE THE TRAY. Before assembly, sand the base sides, base middle, legs and holders to create smooth surfaces and edges. Apply a natural oil finish such as linseed oil to all the parts. To cut the top (E) to size, set the base onto the tileboard, trace around it, then cut just outside the cutting lines with a jig saw. Attach the tileboard to the base with tileboard adhesive **(photo C).** Use a J-roller to distribute pressure evenly on the tileboard after it is placed on the adhesive. Allow the adhesive to set, and sand any overhang smooth with the edges of the base. To reduce any chipping or cracking of the tileboard surface, apply a strip of masking tape along the edges you are sanding. When the adhesive has completely dried, position strips of masking tape across the top, 4½" in from each end. The masking tape strips mark the positions of the holders. Apply a thin bead of adhesive caulk to the undersides of the holders, and clamp the holders to the top so their inside edges are flush with the tape strips **(photo D).** Secure the holders by driving countersunk, 1⅝" deck screws through the base and into the holders **(photo E).** When the caulk has dried, scrape off any excess caulk with a putty knife. Finally, attach a ¾"-dia. rubber foot near each end of both feet.

Once the adhesive caulk has been applied, secure the holders with screws driven up through the base and into the holders.

VACATION HOME FURNISHINGS 77

Gun Cabinet

Keep hunting rifles and ammunition protected and out of sight in this spacious, locking gun cabinet.

PROJECT
POWER TOOLS

A sturdy, clean cabinet equipped with a lock is essential for any hunting lodge or any cabin where firearms are used or stored. The gun cabinet shown here is solid and easy to make. It can hold up to four rifles, and it has six shelves with a separate locking door for storing ammunition. The board-and-batten style cabinet doors can be fitted with just about any kind of lock you choose, depending on your security needs. And the cabinet walls are made from solid pine, so the cabinet looks more like an armoire or pantry than an arsenal.

Structurally, this gun cabinet is basically a pine box held together with cleats on the sides and back. A center stile in front functions as a stop for the cabinet doors. The ammunition rack, built from ¾"-thick plywood, is built separately and inserted inside the cabinet, then fastened in place with wood screws.

Because the cabinet design is so simple, you can alter it to better fit your needs. For example, the ammunition rack can be eliminated, or replaced by a shelf at the top of the cabinet, to create more room for storing additional firearms. If you plan to store the cabinet in an area with high moisture, consider lining the cabinet with tileboard, then caulk the seams and corners and weatherstrip the doors to cut down on moisture penetration inside the cabinet.

Construction Materials

Quantity	Lumber
5	1 × 2" × 8' pine
1	1 × 4" × 6' pine
6	1 × 6" × 6' pine
4	1 × 8" × 8' pine
1	¾" × 4' × 8' plywood
1	¼" × 4' × 8' lauan plywood

78 VACATION HOME FURNISHINGS

OVERALL SIZE:
63½" HIGH
33" WIDE
16" DEEP

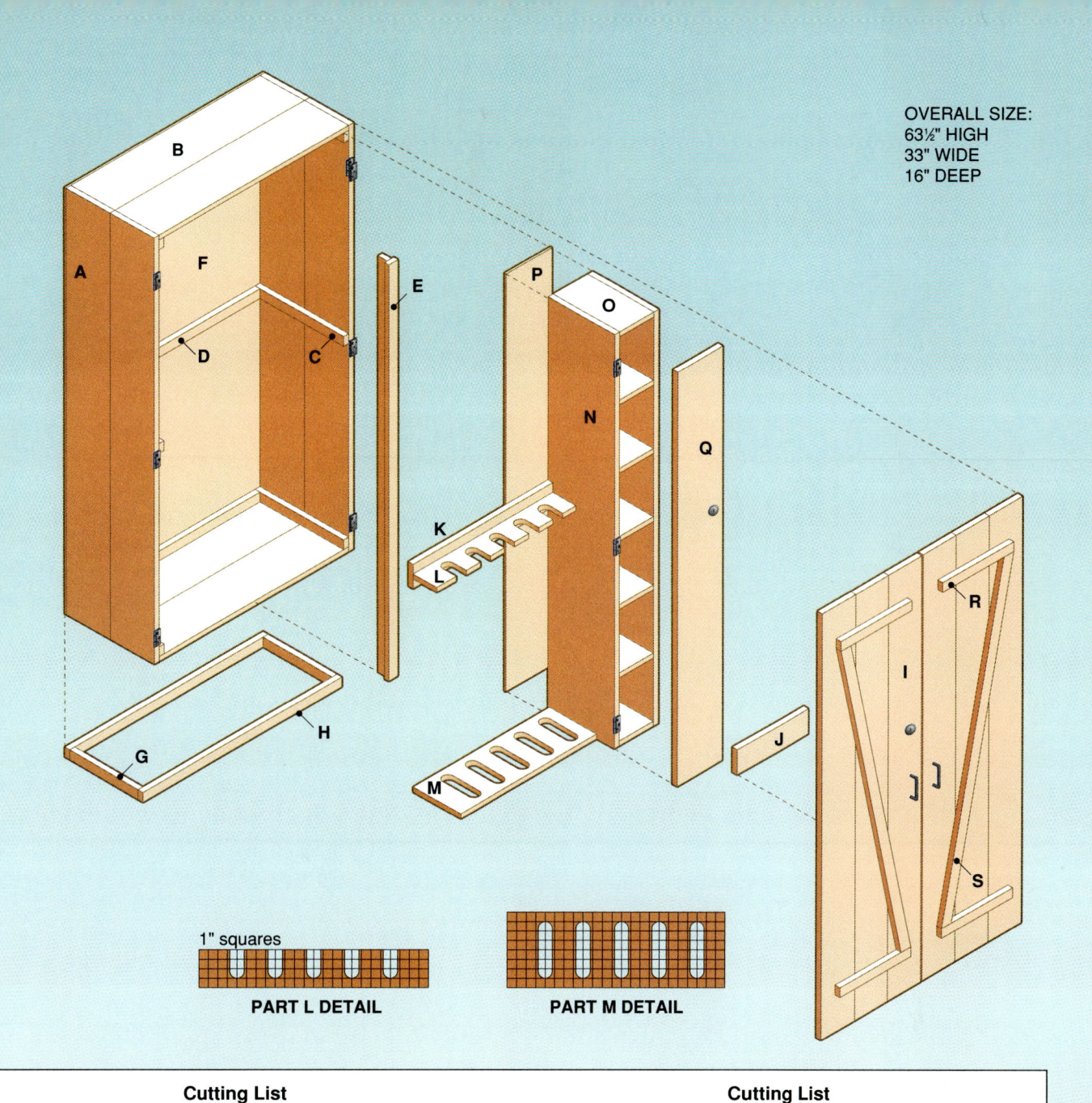

PART L DETAIL

PART M DETAIL

1" squares

Cutting List				
Key	Part	Dimension	Pcs.	Material
A	Side board	¾ × 7¼ × 62"	4	Pine
B	Top/bottom	¾ × 7¼ × 31⅝"	4	Pine
C	Side cleat	¾ × 1½ × 13¾"	6	Pine
D	Back cleat	¾ × 1½ × 31½"	3	Pine
E	Center support	¾ × 1½ × 60½"	2	Pine
F	Back	¼ × 33 × 63½"	1	Lauan plywood
G	Base frame	¾ × 1½ × 11½"	2	Pine
H	Base frame	¾ × 1½ × 33"	2	Pine
I	Door board	¾ × 5½ × 62"	6	Pine
J	Door cleat	¾ × 3½ × 12"	2	Pine

Cutting List				
Key	Part	Dimension	Pcs.	Material
K	Holder back	¾ × 3½ × 23¼"	1	Pine
L	Gun holder	¾ × 4 × 23¼"	1	Plywood
M	Stock receiver	¾ × 8 × 22½"	1	Plywood
N	Storage side	¾ × 11 × 60½"	2	Plywood
O	Cross piece	¾ × 6 × 11"	7	Plywood
P	Storage back	¼ × 7½ × 60½"	1	Lauan plywood
Q	Storage door	¾ × 7½ × 60¼"	1	Plywood
R	Door batten	¾ × 1½ × 12"	2	Pine
S	Door batten	¾ × 1½ × 52"	2	Pine

Materials: Wood glue, #6 wood screws (1", 1¼", 1⅝"), utility hinges: 1½ × 1½" (3); 1½ × 2" (6), 4d finish nails, barrel locks (2), elbow catch, door pulls, finishing materials.

Note: Measurements reflect the actual size of dimensional lumber.

VACATION HOME FURNISHINGS 79

Directions: Gun Cabinet

MAKE THE CABINET SIDES. The sides of the gun cabinet, like the top and bottom panels, are made from solid 1 × 8 pine boards. The boards are held together, edge to edge, with shelf cleats that are attached to the insides and function like board battens. Start by cutting the side boards (A) and side cleats (C) to size. Clamp the side boards together, edge to edge, in groups of two—make sure the ends of the boards are flush. Draw reference lines on the inside faces of the side boards to mark position for the side cleats: the lines should be drawn on the faces of the boards in each pair, ¾" in from each end and ¾" in from one long edge **(photo A).** Also draw a centerline across each set of side boards, 31" from the ends. Position the side cleats on the board pairs. The ends of the cleats should be flush with the line along the long edge to create a ¾" recess for the back-panel cleats (installed later). The cleats should be positioned with their bottom edges flush against the reference lines across the boards. Drill countersunk pilot holes through the side cleats, and attach them with glue and #6 × 1¼" wood screws, driven through the cleats and into the side boards.

ATTACH THE TOP & BOTTOM. Back cleats are attached to the side cleats, connecting the cabinet sides and creating mount-

With the boards for each cabinet side clamped together, mark reference lines for the cabinet top and bottom, and for the back cleats.

Position the back cleats between the cabinet sides, and attach them to the side cleats.

Keep the assembly stable with bar clamps, and fasten the top and bottom boards to the side cleats.

80 VACATION HOME FURNISHINGS

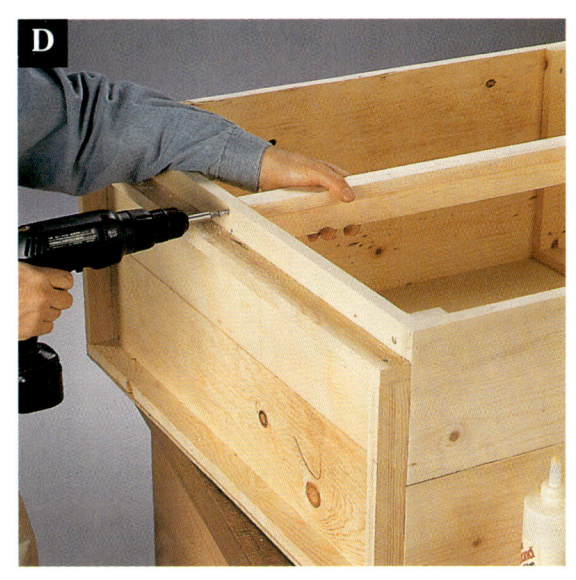

D

Attach the center support, making sure the front face is flush with the front edges of the cabinet.

E

Draw reference lines on the door panels, 5" in from each end, to mark the positions for the horizontal battens on the cabinet doors.

ing surfaces for the back panel. Two top/bottom boards are then fastened to the side cleats, forming the basic cabinet carcase. Begin by cutting the top/bottom boards (B) and back cleats (D) to size. Set the back cleats between the side board assemblies, aligned with the side cleats and butted against the ends. Drill countersunk pilot holes through the back cleats, and attach them to the side cleats with glue and #6 × 1⅝" wood screws **(photo B).** With the assembly laying on its back, position two top/bottom boards between the cabinet sides at the top, and another two at the bottom. Try to make sure the seams between board pairs are aligned with the seams in the sides. Apply glue, and clamp the boards in place at each end, using a bar clamp or pipe clamp. Make sure the cabinet carcase is square, then drive wood screws through the top and bottom boards and into the side cleats **(photo C).**

MAKE THE BASE. The base is a 1 × 2 frame that fits under the bottom of the cabinet to stabilize it and reduce ground contact by the bottom boards. Start by cutting the base frame boards (G, H) to size. Using glue and #6 × 1⅝" wood screws, attach the base sides between the base boards, making sure the outside faces of the base sides are flush with the ends of the base boards. With the cabinet frame on its back, position the rectangular base against one end. The base should be flush with the rear and side edges of the cabinet frame. Mark the base position, and drill pilot holes through the end boards. Attach the base with glue and #6 × 1⅝" wood screws, driven through the end boards and into the base edges.

ATTACH THE BACK PANEL. The back panel for the gun cabinet is made from ¼"-thick lauan plywood. Cut the back panel (F) to size using a circular saw and a straightedge cutting guide. To make sure the back panel is square, measure diagonally from corner to corner. If the measurements are the same, the back is square—this is important because the back panel is used to square-up the cabinet carcase. Lay the cabinet down on its front edges, and set the back over the rear edges of the side boards and the back cleats. Tack the back panel at the corners, making sure it is flush with the outside edges of the cabinet all the way around. Drive 1" wire brads every 6" into the sides and back cleats to attach the back panel.

INSTALL THE CENTER SUPPORT. The center support fits in the front of the cabinet opening, running from top to bottom, to create a stile that works as a center door stop. Cut the two center support (E) pieces from 1 × 2 pine, then butt the long edge of one board against the face of the other board to form a "T" shape. Make sure the parts are flush at the ends, then join them with glue and 4d finish nails. Turn the cabinet over on its back, and position the center support in the center of the front opening. The face of the center support assembly should be directed forward, flush with the front of the

VACATION HOME FURNISHINGS 81

For accuracy, use a sliding T-bevel to measure and transfer the angle where the battens meet.

Position a cross piece between the storage sides at each end of the ammunition rack, and attach the parts with glue and screws.

cabinet. Drill pilot holes through the top and bottom boards, and attach the center support with glue and two #6 × 1⅝" wood screws driven at each end **(photo D).**

MAKE THE CABINET DOORS. The cabinet doors are each made with three 1 × 6 boards fitted with 1 × 2 battens, arranged in a "Z" shape, to hold the two boards together. Begin by cutting the door boards (I), door cleats (J), and door battens (R, S). Set the door boards on your worksurface, edge-to-edge, in sets of three. Use a framing square to make sure the door boards are square and flush at their ends. Clamp each set of door boards together with pipe or bar clamps. Draw reference lines across the door boards, 5" in from each end, to mark position for the horizontal battens **(photo E).** Set the horizontal battens just inside the reference lines, centered side to side, and attach them with glue and #6 × 1¼" wood screws.

Note: for a more finished appearance, drive the screws through the back faces of the door panels and into the battens. Mark the diagonal battens to fit between opposite ends of the horizontal battens on each door: the most accurate way to do this is to use a sliding T-bevel to transfer the angle of intersection onto the battens **(photo F).** Or, if you are not too concerned about precision, you can simply lay the the vertical batten strips in position and draw cutting lines that approximately follow the inside edges of the horizontal battens. Cut the vertical batten strips along the cutting lines with a jig saw or circular saw (or a power miter saw if you own one). Attach the strips to the doors with glue and wood screws. Flip the doors over on their fronts. Center a door cleat across the back of each door, and attach it with #6 × 1" wood screws.

MAKE THE AMMUNITION RACK. The ammunition rack is built as a unit and inserted into the

cabinet. Because the rack has its own door, you can equip it with its own lock for extra protection. Begin by cutting the storage sides (N), cross pieces (O) and storage back (P) to size. Position the storage sides on-edge on a flat worksurface. Glue and clamp two cross pieces between them at each end. Turn the assembly on its side, and drive 4d finish nails through the storage sides and into the cross pieces **(photo G).** Attach the storage back with glue and wire brads. Draw reference lines on the storage sides to mark the positions of the remaining cross pieces. We marked lines every 9" up the length of the ammunition rack. Apply glue to the sides of the cross pieces, and slide them in place. Check with a square to make sure the cross pieces are square to the storage sides, and attach them with 4d finish nails. Place the ammunition rack inside the main cabinet (we positioned it on the right-hand side). Make sure it is flush

82 VACATION HOME FURNISHINGS

Cut holes in the stock receiver with a holesaw, then connect the holes with a jigsaw, forming notches to hold the gun stocks.

against the back and one side of the cabinet. Attach it by driving wood screws through the top and bottom of the cabinet and into the storage sides. Cut the storage door (Q) to size, and attach it to the innermost storage side with three 1½ × 1½" butt hinges.

MAKE THE GUN RACK. The gun rack consists of a pair of boards that are notched to hold the stock and the barrel of each gun. The boards are installed at the bottom and the center of the cabinet. Cut the gun holder (L), holder back (K) and stock receiver (M) to size from ¾"-thick plywood. Lay out the cutouts on the gun holder and stock receiver according to the *Part L Detail* and *Part M Detail* on page 79. Make the rounded ends of the cutouts with a 1½"-dia. holesaw installed in your electric drill, and use a jig saw to connect the holes, completing the cutouts **(photo H)**. Sand the edges to smooth out any rough spots. Butt the gun holder against one face of the holder back. Make sure the gun holder is centered and that the open ends of the grooves face away from the holder back. Attach the gun holder with glue and wood screws, driven through the holder back and into the gun holder edge. Fit the assembly into the cabinet, flush against the back and the middle back cleat. Glue the holder back in place, and attach it with #6 × 1" wood screws driven through the back panel and into the assembly. Position the stock receiver on the floor of the cabinet, flush against the back. Attach the stock receiver with glue and #6 × 1" wood screws.

INSTALL THE HARDWARE. Hang the cabinet doors on the cabinet with 1½ × 2" butt hinges attached to the front edges of the cabinet sides. Use three hinges for each door, positioned in the middle and about 4" in from the top and the bottom of the cabinet. We installed barrel locks in the storage door for the ammunition rack and in the cabinet door, according to the lock manufacturer's instructions (we added an elbow catch inside the cabinet door that did not receive the barrel lock). Barrel locks are sufficient to keep young children out of the cabinets, but if higher security is important to you, use a sturdy hasp and padlock instead. Also attach door pulls to each cabinet door (because we installed a barrel lock on the ammunition rack door, we didn't feel that a pull was necessary—if you do not install a lock, cut a finger grip slot in the door with your jig saw).

APPLY FINISHING TOUCHES. Set all nail heads with a nail set, then fill all the screw and nail holes with wood putty. After it dries, sand the putty level with the surrounding wood. Finish-sand all the wood surfaces with medium grit, then fine grit sandpaper. Wipe with a rag dipped in mineral spirits, then apply your finish of choice after the wood dries. We simply applied two coats of water-based polyurethane for a protective coat that hardens the wood. If you prefer to paint your gun cabinet, be sure to use primer and a good-quality enamel paint. To protect your guns while they are in the cabinet, cut strips of felt and glue them around the cutouts in the gun holder and stock receiver, using contact cement. A layer of felt at the bottom of each stock receiver cutout is also a good idea. For best results and maximum safety, find a cool, dry and well-protected area to keep your gun cabinet. Do not place it near heat sources or in high traffic areas.

PROJECT
POWER TOOLS

Suitcase Stand

Living out of a suitcase is a little more bearable with this sturdy, convenient suitcase stand that folds up for easy storage.

Construction Materials	
Quantity	**Lumber**
2	1 × 4" × 6' pine
3	2 × 4" × 8' pine
1	1 × 10" × 6' pine
4	¾"-dia. × 3' hardwood dowel

Perfect for a guest bedroom or a front hallway in your vacation home, this suitcase stand adds a touch of hospitality and convenience to any living area. Made from pine and hardwood dowels, this fold-up stand is easy and economical to build. The gate-leg design allows you to fold up the leg assemblies so the stand fits neatly into a closet or under a bed. But if your vacation home is like most, the sturdiness and efficient size of this suitcase stand will soon have it doing permanent duty as an extra table.

84 VACATION HOME FURNISHINGS

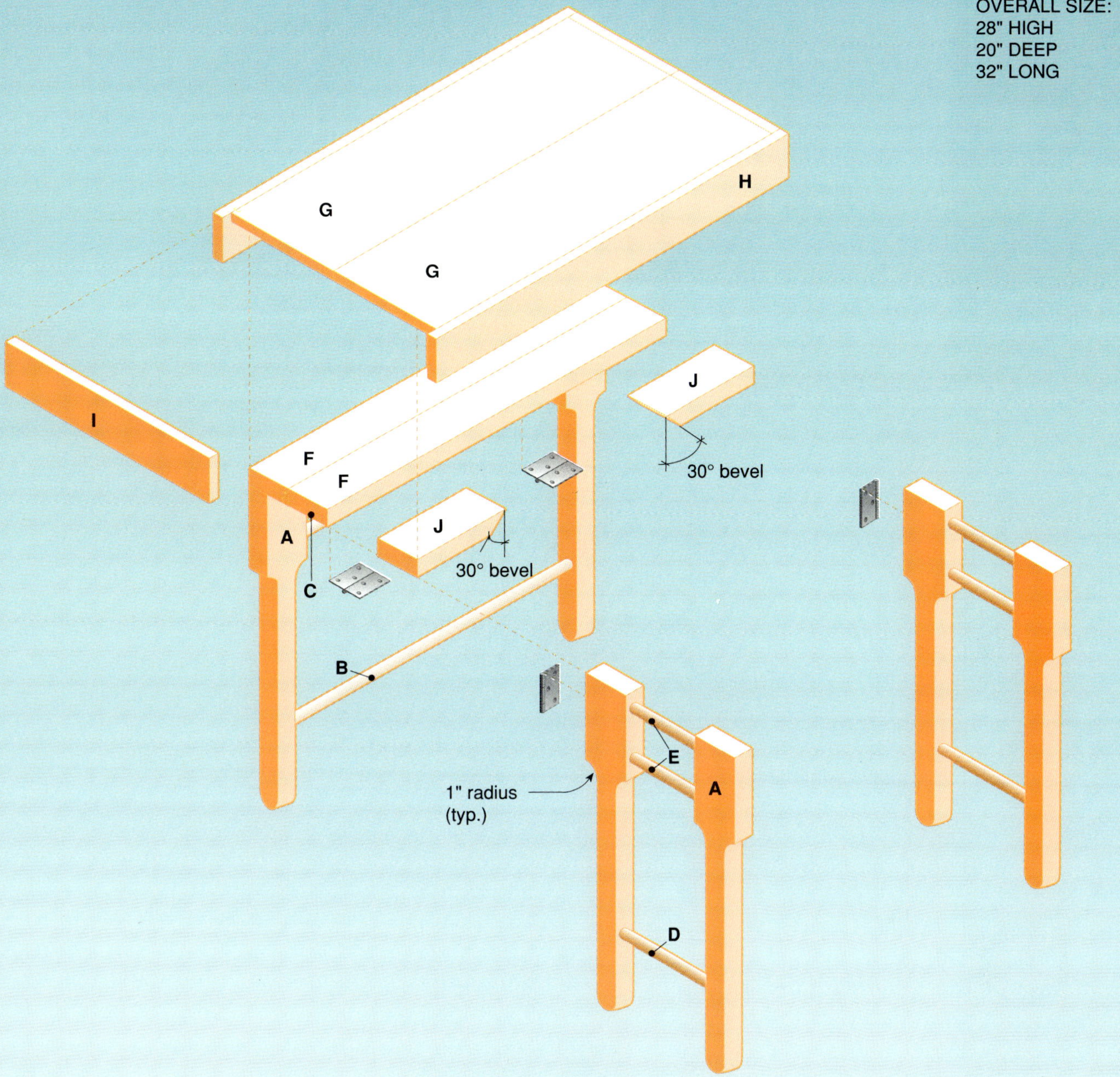

OVERALL SIZE:
28" HIGH
20" DEEP
32" LONG

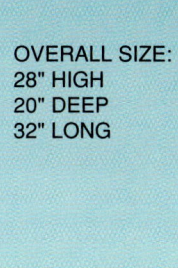

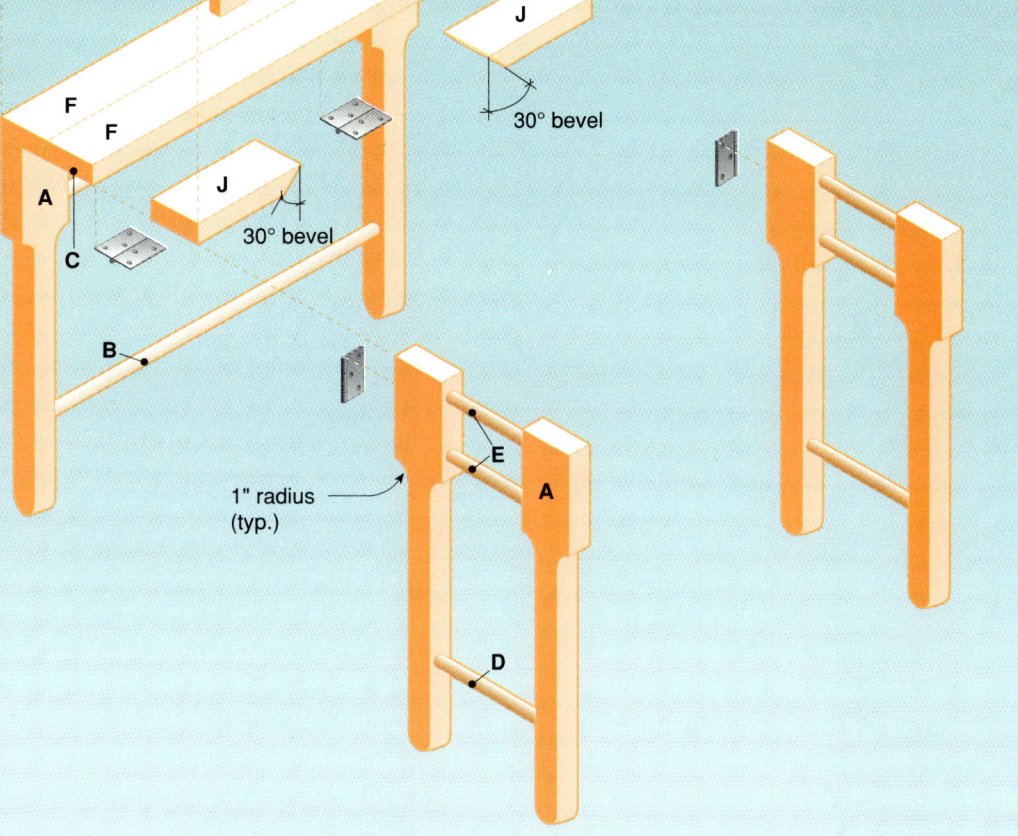

Cutting List			
Key	Part	Dimension	Pcs.	Material
A	Leg	1½ × 3½ × 25¾"	6	Pine
B	Back stretcher	¾"-dia. × 26½"	1	Hardwood dowel
C	Back stretcher	¾"-dia. × 24½"	2	Hardwood dowel
D	Gate stretcher	¾"-dia. × 9½"	2	Hardwood dowel
E	Gate stretcher	¾"-dia. × 7½"	4	Hardwood dowel

Cutting List			
Key	Part	Dimension	Pcs.	Material
F	Back brace	1½ × 3½ × 30½"	2	Pine
G	Top board	¾ × 9½ × 30½"	2	Pine
H	Side board	¾ × 3½ × 32"	2	Pine
I	End board	¾ × 3½ × 18½"	2	Pine
J	Gate rest	1½ × 3½ × 8"	2	Pine

Materials: Wood screws (#6 × 2", #6 × 2½"), finish nails (6d), wood glue, finishing materials.

Note: Measurements reflect the actual thickness of dimensional lumber.

VACATION HOME FURNISHINGS 85

A

Position the side boards against the top boards and end boards, and fasten them with glue and screws.

B

Position the beveled gate rests against opposite end boards, and fasten them to the top boards.

Directions: Suitcase Stand

MAKE THE TOP. The top is made by butting two boards together, edge to edge, and wrapping them on all sides with a 1 × 4 apron frame. The top is then turned upside down, and beveled boards, which support the leg assemblies, are attached inside the frame. Start by cutting the top boards (G), side boards (H) and end boards (I) to size. Sand the boards after cutting to smooth out any rough spots. Position the top boards edge to edge on your worksurface with their ends flush. Butt the end boards against the ends of the top boards. Drill evenly spaced pilot holes, counterbored to accept ⅜"-dia. wood plugs, and attach the end boards to the top boards with glue and #6 × 2" wood screws. Position the side boards against the top boards and end boards, and fasten them with glue and counterbored wood screws, driven through the side boards and into the end boards and top boards **(photo A)**. Glue ⅜"-dia. wood plugs into all counterbores in the top, then, when the glue has dried, sand the plugs flush with the surrounding wood. Round the corners and edges of the assembly with a sander. Cut the back braces (F) and gate rests (J) to size. Set one back brace aside to use in the leg construction. Use a power miter box or a belt sander to make a 30° bevel at one end of each gate rest. This bevel allows the gates to slide onto the gate rests when the suitcase stand is assembled. Butt the square ends of the gate rests against the opposite end boards, making sure the bevels on the gate rests are facing away from the top boards. The outside edges of the gate rests should be 1¾" in from a common side board. Attach the gate rests with glue and #6 × 2" wood screws **(photo B)**. Position a back brace facedown in the top frame, 5¼" in from the side board opposite the gate rests, and attach it with glue and wood screws. Apply a stain to the top, and seal the color with a clear oil finish.

C

Once the patterns have been traced onto the legs, cut the leg shapes with a jig saw.

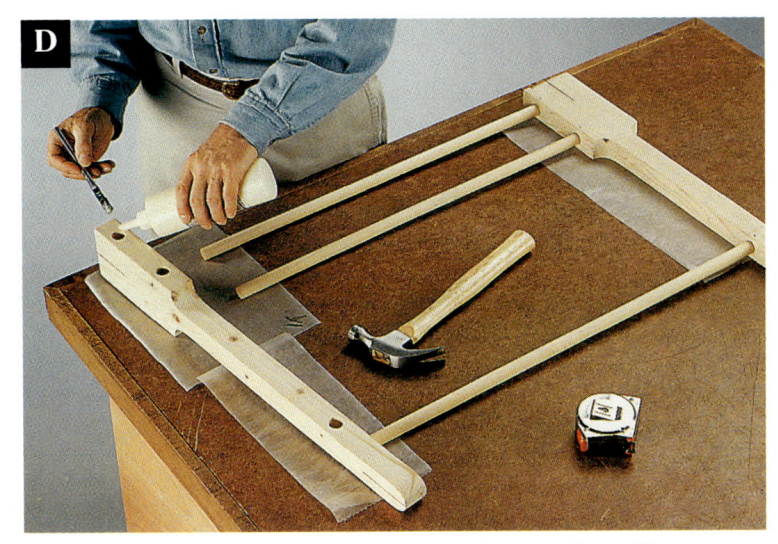

Apply glue in the dowel holes, then insert the stretchers. To prevent spinning, drive 6d finish nails through the legs and into the stretchers.

Attach the two gate stretcher assemblies to the back stretcher assembly with utility hinges.

MAKE THE LEGS. Six 2 × 4 boards are cut to shape to form the legs. When the legs are organized in pairs and fastened together with dowel stretchers, they form the hinged assemblies that support the top. Cut the legs (A) to length. Designate a top and bottom of each leg. To draw the cutting lines for the leg profiles, mark two 19"-long reference lines on each leg face, 1" in from each long edge. Use a compass to draw a 1"-radius semicircle at the top of each reference line. Use a jig saw to cut the legs to shape **(photo C).** Use a ¾"-dia. drum sander attachment for your electric drill to sand the legs smooth, and round over the bottoms of the legs. Drill ¾"-deep × ¾"-dia. dowel holes into the narrow edges of each leg. (Place a piece of tape on your drill bit to act as a depth stop.) Center the holes 6" up from the bottoms of the legs, and 1⅜" and 5⅜" down from the top of each leg.

ATTACH THE STRETCHERS. Dowel stretchers are inserted into the holes in the legs, forming three stretcher assemblies. The largest of these assemblies, the back stretcher assembly, is hinged to the bottom of the table. The two gate assemblies are then hinged to the back stretcher assembly, allowing the legs to fold into the apron frame. Cut the back stretchers (B, C) and gate stretchers (D, E) to length. Test-fit the back stretchers between a pair of legs. (The dowel holes should be deep enough to allow for adjustment.) The long back stretcher (B) fits into the lowest dowel holes. Before permanently fastening the stretchers, turn the top frame upside down and position the assembly in the top frame so the outside edges of the legs butt squarely against the end boards (I). Make reference marks on the stretchers where they enter the dowel holes. Remove the assembly from the top frame. Apply glue into the dowel holes, then insert the stretchers into the holes, using the reference marks as guides **(photo D).** Also glue the gate stretchers into the appropriate dowel holes. Secure the stretchers with 6d finish nails driven through the legs and into the stretchers. Apply stain and topcoat to the leg assemblies to match (or contrast, as we did) the finish on the tabletop.

APPLY FINISHING TOUCHES. Position the unattached back brace on edge on your worksurface. Set the back stretcher assembly on the back brace, flush with the ends and one long edge. Drill pilot holes, and fasten the workpieces with glue and countersunk #6 × 2½" wood screws, driven through the back brace and into the tops of the legs. Set the back brace edge to edge against the back brace that is already attached in the top frame. Attach the back braces with two evenly spaced 1½ × 3" utility hinges. Position the gate stretcher assemblies against the back stretcher assembly, and clamp them in place. Make sure the outside faces of the gate stretcher assemblies are touching the end boards, and attach the gate stretcher assemblies to the back stretcher assembly with 1½ × 3" utility hinges **(photo E),** positioned 2" down from the tops of the legs.

PROJECT
POWER TOOLS

Boot Dryer

Hiking or biking, skiing or just working outdoors, nothing beats the feeling of slipping into a pair of warm, dry boots.

Construction Materials	
Quantity	**Lumber**
4	1 × 2" × 8' pine
1	1 × 4" × 8' pine
2	2 × 2" × 8' pine

You may not want to display this boot dryer in the middle of your cabin when company comes to visit, but if you've ever had to don a pair of damp boots on a cold morning, you'll appreciate what it can do for you.

The boot spindles are designed to support your boots (as many as eight pairs at a time) in optimal drying position, well above the ground. The open design leaves plenty of space for air to circulate—for fast drying, set up the boot dryer near a heat register or even a fireplace.

When the boot dryer is not needed, it folds up flat so it can be stored in just about any closet.

88 VACATION HOME FURNISHINGS

OVERALL SIZE:
48" HIGH
18" WIDE
16" DEEP

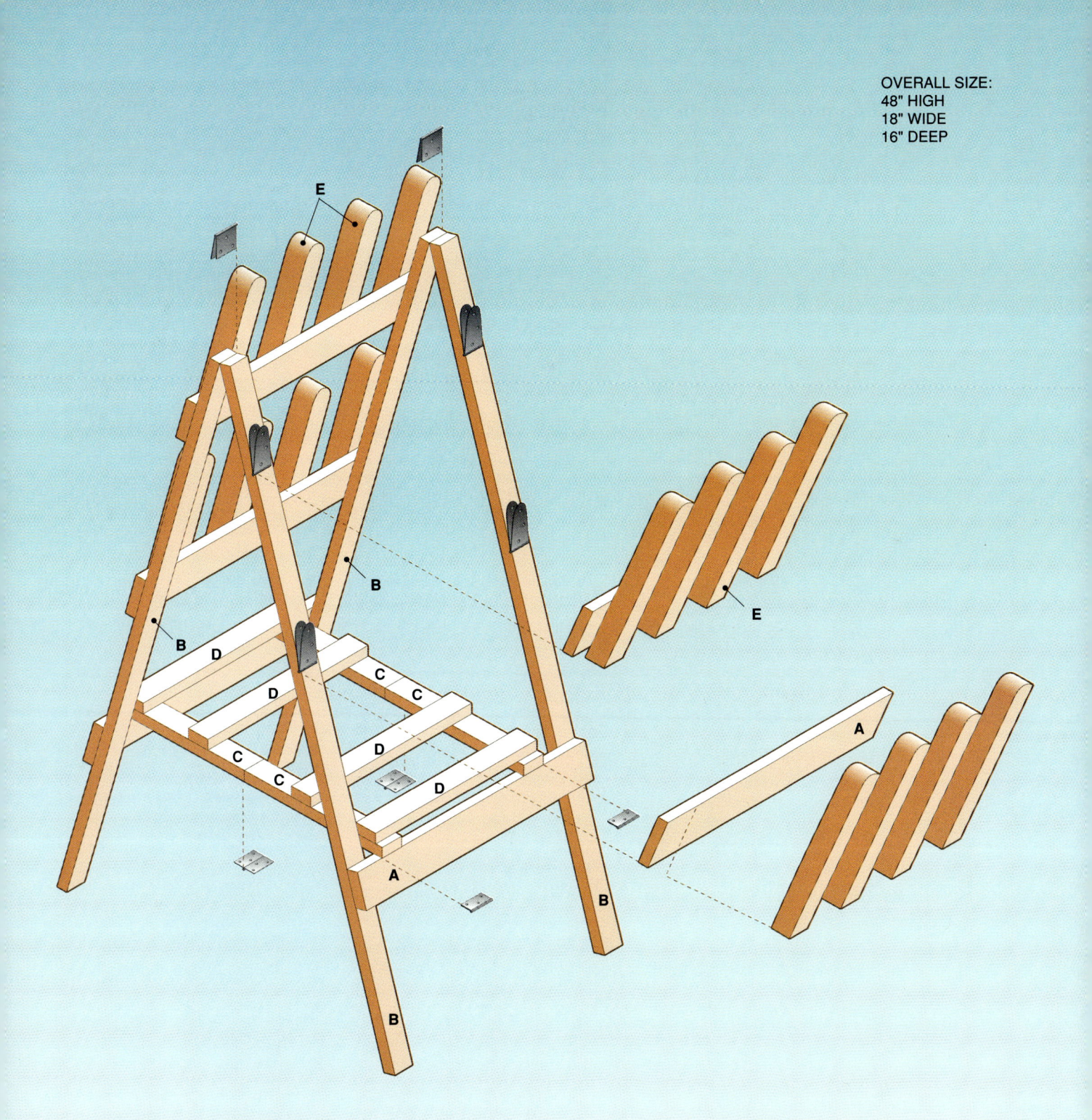

| Cutting List ||||
Key	Part	Dimension	Pcs.	Material
A	Hinge rail	¾ × 3½ × 15⅞"	6	Pine
B	Leg	¾ × 1½ × 49"	4	Pine
C	Center slat	¾ × 1½ × 9"	4	Pine

| Cutting List ||||
Key	Part	Dimension	Pcs.	Material
D	Cross slat	¾ × 1½ × 12½"	4	Pine
E	Boot spindle	1½ × 1½ × 11⅞"	16	Pine

Materials: Glue, wood screws (#6 × 1¼", #6 × 2"), 1½ × 3" strap hinges (10), 1½ × 1½" utility hinges (6), finishing materials.

Note: Measurements reflect the actual thickness of dimensional lumber.

VACATION HOME FURNISHINGS 89

A

Use a piece of scrap wood as a stop to help you align the strap hinge barrels so they are flush with the ends of the hinge rails.

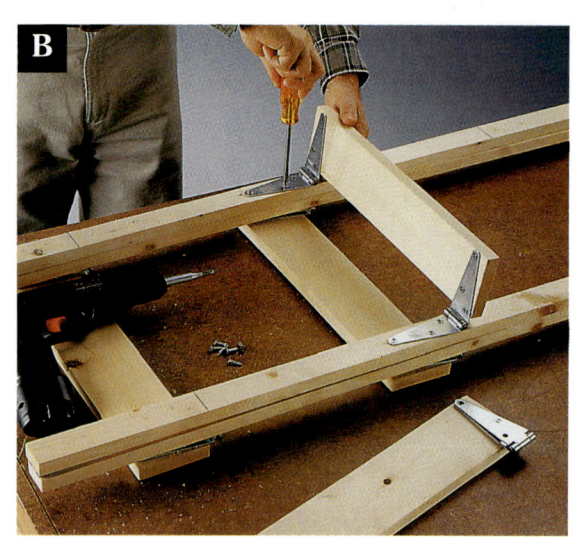

B

Attach the top hinge rails to the legs so their bottom edges are flush with the reference lines.

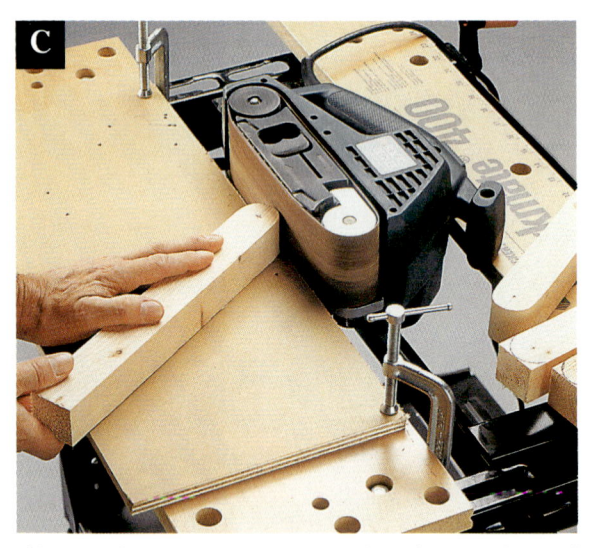

C

Clamp a belt sander to your worksurface, and round over one end of each boot spindle.

Directions: Boot Dryer

MAKE THE HINGE RAILS. The hinge rails are the crosspieces that are used to secure the boot spindles. Start by cutting the hinge rails (A) to length. Sand all parts after cutting to smooth out any rough spots. Use #6 × 1¼" wood screws to fasten pairs of 1½ × 1½" utility hinges to two of the hinge rails: the utility hinges should be attached along one edge of each board, 1⅝" in from each end. The hinge barrels should not overhang past the edges of the rails. On the two remaining hinge rails, position a pair of 1½ × 3" heavy-duty strap hinges on one face of each rail. The hinges should be flush with the ends of the rails. To make sure they are flush, press a piece of scrap wood against the end of each rail to make stops for the hinges. Fasten the strap hinges with #6 × 1¼" wood screws **(photo A)**.

MAKE THE LEGS. Two pairs of legs are joined together into a folding A-frame assembly. Cut the legs (B) to size. Sand the legs, then position them against each other edge to edge on your worksurface. Make sure the ends of the legs are flush, and draw reference lines across the legs 8" and 21½" in from the one end, and 14½" in from the other end (these lines mark position for the hinge rails). Butt the ends of two legs together, and attach a 1½ × 3" strap hinge over the joint. The barrel of the strap hinge should be facing away from the legs. Fasten the hinges with wood screws. Repeat the process to make the other leg pair.

ATTACH THE TOP HINGE RAILS. Start by folding the leg pairs into closed positions. Set the leg pairs on your worksurface 16" apart. Position the hinge rails with the attached strap hinges so their bottom edges are flush with the top two reference lines (8" and 21") on the legs, and attach the free hinge plate **(photo B)**. The hinge rails should fold upward against the legs when they are attached.

MAKE THE BOOT SPINDLES. The boot spindles, which hold the boots in place, are attached to the top hinge rails. Cut the boot spindles (E) to length. To round over the tips of the spindles, draw a ¾"-radius curve at one end of each boot leg, using a compass or a scrap of 1½"-dia. pipe as a guide. Clamp a belt sander to your worksurface so the belt is vertical, then use a medium-grit sanding belt to shape the spindle ends **(photo C)**. Make all of the spindles. Position a boot spindle at one end of a hinge rail, making sure its outside edge is flush with the end of the hinge rail. The bottom of the spindle should extend 1½" below the bottom edge of the hinge rail. (If needed, draw reference lines 1½" up from the bottoms of the spindles to help you position them correctly.) Drill countersunk pilot holes, and attach the spindle to the hinge rail with glue and two #6 × 2" wood screws. Attach the rest of the spindles in position (see *Diagram,* page 89), using a 3⅜"-wide piece of scrap wood as a spacer between spindles **(photo D).**

MAKE THE SHELF. The shelf fits in the bottom of the boot dryer, helping to keep it stable. When the dryer is completed, the shelf will fold out between the leg pairs when the legs are extended, and fold up flat when the legs are collapsed. Begin by cutting the center slats (C) and cross slats (D) to size. Arrange the center slats in pairs so their ends are flush. With the center slats positioned edge to edge, draw reference lines ½" and 5½" in from one end of each slat. Set a pair of cross slats on the center slat pairs so the outside edge of each cross slat is flush with the reference lines. Make sure the ends of the cross slats are flush with the edges of the center slats. Drill pilot holes, and attach the cross slats with glue and #6 × 1¼" wood screws, driven through the cross slats and into the center slats. Turn the two frames upside down so the cross slats are on your worksurface, and butt them together so the ½"-wide gap is on the outside. Join the frames with 1½ × 1½" utility hinges. The barrels of the hinges should face away from the center slats. For now, remove the hinges. Position the remaining hinge rails on the legs so their top edges are flush with the reference lines, 14½" up from the bottoms of the legs. Make sure the utility hinges are on the top edge of the hinge rails, with the barrels facing out, and fasten the hinge rails with glue and #6 × 1¼" wood screws. Set the frame on its side, and attach the shelf frames to the hinge rails, fastening the unattached hinge plates to the center slats. (The hinges should be attached to the center slat faces opposite the cross slats.) Fold the shelf frames between the legs, and reattach them with 1½ × 1½" utility hinges **(photo E).** Open and close the boot rack to make sure it operates correctly. We painted the boot dryer with primer and enamel paint, but if you prefer you can simply apply a protective finish, like polyurethane, to the wood.

Use a piece of scrap to maintain even spacing as you attach the boot spindles to the hinge rails.

Fasten the shelf racks together with utility hinges, making sure the hinge barrels are facing the bottoms of the legs.

Rod & Tackle Center

PROJECT POWER TOOLS

This two-sided equipment storage center can hold up to eight fishing rods, plus spare tackle and a pair of tackle boxes.

Anyone who loves to fish knows how problematic fishing rod storage can be. Lines become tangled together; rods tip over and spill out from corners in all directions; fragile (and expensive) reels poke out into traffic areas, where they are vulnerable to kicking and bumping; and worst of all, hooks and lures can creep out dangerously into your living spaces. With this simple storage center, you can keep your fishing rods and tackle well organized, tangle-free and out of harm's way.

Designed with a sleek profile so it fits against a wall, this rod & tackle center makes efficient use of your space. The slide-out tackle tray and the open tackle box storage area can be accessed from either side. The rod racks feature cutouts in both the upper and lower racks so rods will not slip out or rub together.

The rod & tackle center can be positioned flat against the wall to consume the minimum amount of floor space, or you can set it with a side panel against the wall for maximum accessibility. Either way, at least one side panel will be exposed so you can attach hooks for hanging landing nets or even your favorite fishing hat.

Construction Materials

Quantity	Lumber
1	¾" × 4 × 8' plywood
1	¼" × 2 × 2' lauan plywood

92 VACATION HOME FURNISHINGS

OVERALL SIZE:
69" HIGH
20" WIDE
13½" DEEP

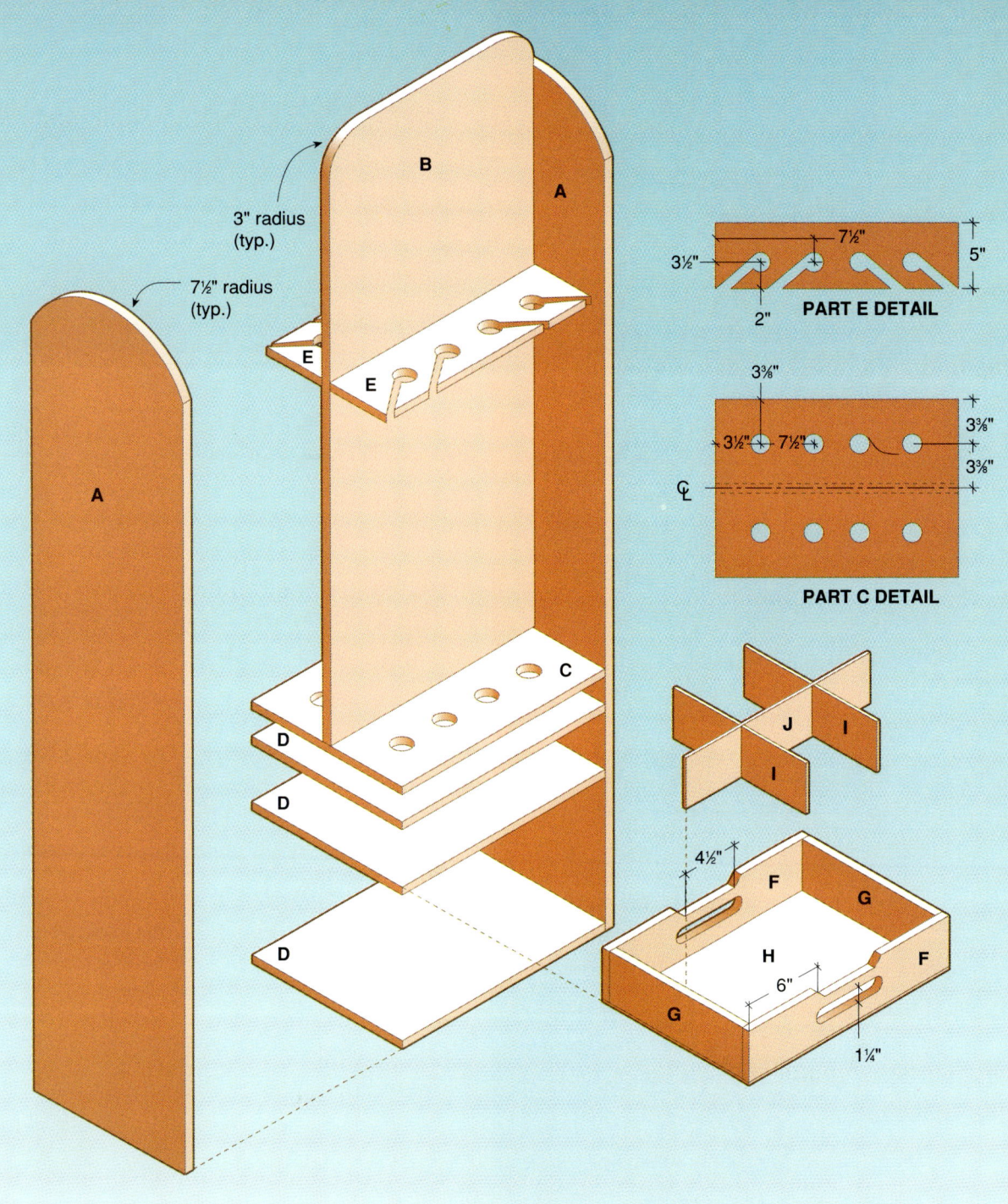

PART E DETAIL

PART C DETAIL

Cutting List					Cutting List			
Key	Part	Dimension	Pcs.	Material	Key	Part	Dimension	Pcs.	Material
A	Side	¾ × 13½ × 65¼"	2	Plywood	F	Tray front/back	¾ × 4⅛ × 18¼"	2	Plywood
B	Divider	¾ × 18½ × 48"	1	Plywood	G	Tray side	¾ × 4⅛ × 11½"	2	Plywood
C	Lower rack	¾ × 13½ × 18½"	1	Plywood	H	Tray bottom	¼ × 13 × 18¼"	1	Lauan plywood
D	Shelf	¾ × 13½ × 18½"	3	Plywood	I	Short tray divider	¼ × 4 × 11½"	2	Lauan plywood
E	Upper rack	¾ × 5 × 18½"	2	Plywood	J	Long tray divider	¼ × 4 × 16¾"	1	Lauan plywood

Materials: Glue, #6 × 1⅝" deck screws, ¾" wire brads, finishing materials.

Note: Measurements reflect the actual thickness of dimensional lumber.

VACATION HOME FURNISHINGS

A

Use a jig saw to cut the 7½"-radius curves on the tops of the side panels.

Directions: Rod & Tackle Center

MAKE THE SIDES. The sides are the standards that support the shelves and racks in the rod & tackle center. They feature decorative roundovers on top to make the appearance less bulky. Start by cutting the sides (A) to size from ¾"-thick plywood (we used birch plywood because it's easier to work with and finish than most grades of pine plywood). Draw a 7½"-radius roundover at the top of each side panel. If you don't have a compass that is large enough to draw a curve that big, make one yourself: first, cut a narrow strip of scrap wood about 10" long. Then, mark a centerpoint on the scrap near one end, and another 7½" in from the first point. Drill a ¼"-dia. hole at the first centerpoint, and drill a small pilot hole at the second point. Next, mark a centerpoint on each side panel, 7½" down from the top and centered side to side. Drive a finish nail through the small pilot hole in the compass and into one of the side panels at the centerpoint. Insert a pencil into the ¼"-dia. hole, and draw the roundover using the finish nail as a pivot point. Draw roundovers on both side panels. Cut along the roundover lines on both panels with a jig saw **(photo A)**. Sand out any rough spots on the side panels.

ATTACH THE SHELVES. The rod & tackle center has four shelves installed near the bottom. The bottom shelf is flush with the bottoms of the side panels; the second shelf supports the sliding tray; the third shelf supports the ends of the fishing rod handles; and the fourth shelf features round cutouts to hold the handles in place. Start by cutting the lower rack (C) and shelves (D) to size. Mark centerpoints for two rows of four

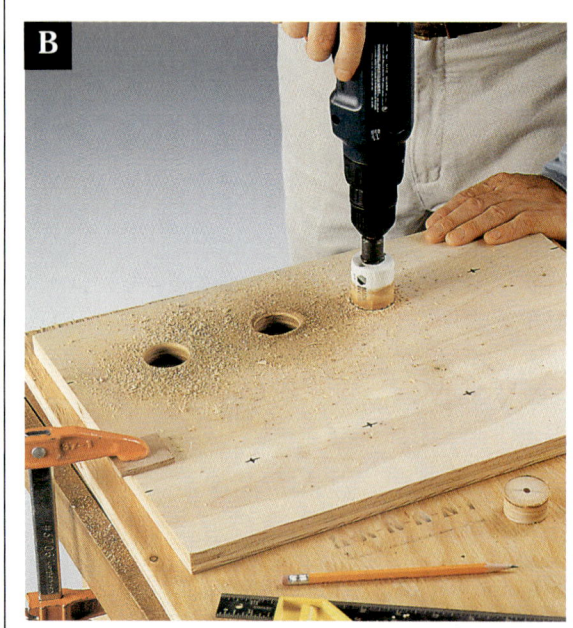

B

Use a 1½"-dia. hole saw attachment in your drill to cut evenly spaced holes in the lower rack.

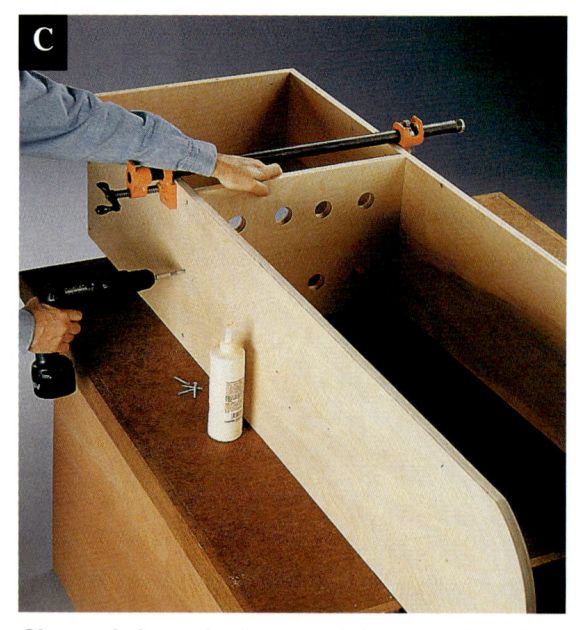

C

Glue and clamp the lower rack between the sides, then reinforce the joint with wood screws.

1½"-dia. holes on the lower shelf, according to the positioning shown on the *Part C Detail* on page 93. Cut the holes with a 1½"-dia. hole saw attachment and drill **(photo B).** Set the sides on edge, about 20" apart. Apply glue to the edges of one shelf, and position it between the sides so the bottom face is flush with the bottom edges of the sides. Drill countersunk pilot holes, and drive #6 × 1⅝" wood screws through the sides and into the shelf. Next, glue and clamp the lower rack between the sides, 20" up from the bottoms. Drive #6 × 1⅝" wood screws to reinforce the joint **(photo C).** Install the remaining two crosspieces with glue and countersunk deck screws. The bottoms should be 12" and 17½" up from the bottoms of the side panels.

INSTALL THE DIVIDER. The divider fits between the side panels, resting on top of the lower rack. Cut the divider (B) to size. Use a compass to draw 3"-radius roundovers on both corners at one end (the top) of the divider. Cut the roundovers with a jig saw. Apply beads of glue to the bottom (square) edge of the divider and the outer edges, then position it so it is centered between the side panels, front to back, and resting squarely on the top of the lower rack. Clamp the divider between the sides with pipe clamps or bar clamps **(photo D),** then drive wood screws through countersunk pilot holes in the side panels and into the edges of the divider—space the screws at 8" intervals.

INSTALL THE UPPER RACKS. The upper racks are installed on each side of the divider to create slip-in supports for the

Clamp the side panels around the divider after you install the shelves and lower rack.

Lay out the angled slots that connect the holes to the front edges of the upper racks, where the tips of your fishing rods will fit.

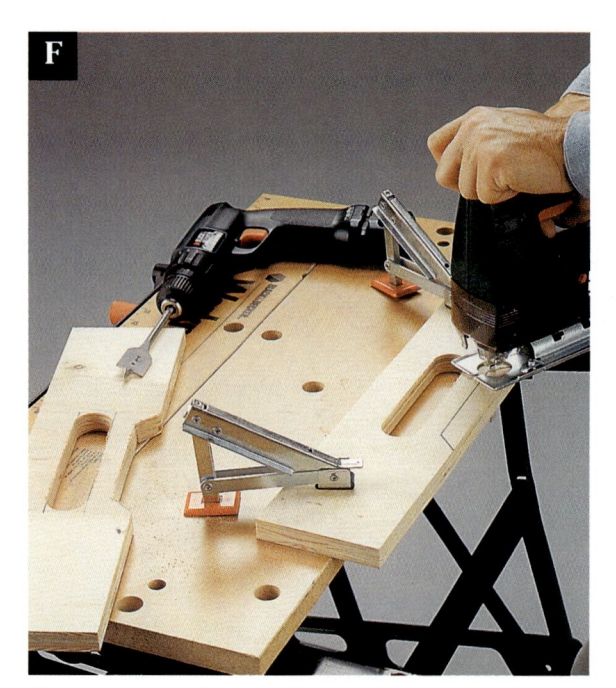

Cut access notches and finger-grip cutouts into the front and back boards of the tray.

The tray dividers are notched to form half-lap joints—test to make sure they fit together before you glue them into the tray.

tips of the fishing rods. Both upper rack boards have a row of four 1½"-dia. holes, with an angled slot cut from the front edge of each board to each hole so you can slip the fishing rod into the hole. Cut the upper racks (E) to size, and mark centerpoints for four evenly spaced 1½" holes in each shelf, according to the spacing shown in *Part E Detail* on page 93. Also draw cutting lines to mark angled, ½"-wide slots from the front edge of each rack to each hole **(photo E).** Cut the slots with a jig saw. To attach the upper racks, mark straight reference lines on both faces of the divider, 28" up from the lower rack. Position the upper racks between the side panels so the tops are flush with the reference lines. Make sure the upper racks butt flush against the divider. Drill countersunk pilot holes through the sides, and attach the upper racks with glue and countersunk #6 × 1⅝" wood screws driven through the sides and into the ends of the racks.

MAKE THE TRAY BOX. The box that serves as the tackle tray has a front and back with access notches and slots for finger-grips. Cut the tray front/back boards (F), the tray sides (G) and the tray bottom (H). Mark a centerline on the faces of the front and back boards, measuring from end to end. Draw a 1¼"-high × 6¼"-long cutout on each board. The tip of the cutout should be 2¼" down from the top of the board. Use a drill with a 1¼" spade bit to create the rounded ends of the cut, then connect the holes with a jig saw to form the slot on each board. Then, cut a ¾"-deep notch in the top edge, centered on the centerline, starting 6" in from each end of the board. The sides of the notch should angle in at about 45° **(photo F).** Drill pilot holes, and attach the tray sides between the tray front and back with glue and #6 × 1⅝" wood screws, forming a rectangular frame. Attach the tray bottom to the frame with glue and ¾" wire brads.

INSTALL THE TRAY DIVIDER. The tray dividers are made from thin lauan plywood, cut in strips that fit together with half-lap joints. Cut the tray dividers (I, J) to size from ¼"-thick lauan plywood. Use a jig saw to cut a ¼"-wide × 2"-long notch in the center of each of the two shorter dividers (I). Cut a pair of ¼"-wide × 2"-long notches in the longer divider (J), 5¼" in from each end. Fit a short divider notch over each long divider notch to make sure the parts fit together **(photo G)**, then glue them in place in the bottom of the tray.

APPLY FINISHING TOUCHES. Fill all screw holes with putty. Finish-sand the entire project, and apply a paint and primer finish. Paint the tray section separately, then insert it in the shelf area when the finish has completely dried.